Frederick County
CHRONICLES

Frederick County
CHRONICLES

The Crossroads of Maryland

MARIE ANNE ERICKSON

EDITED *by* INGRID PRICE

FOREWORD *by* CHRISTOPHER HAUGH

THE History PRESS

Published by The History Press
Charleston, SC 29403
www.historypress.net

Front cover, top: Yellow Springs Band. *Courtesy of the Historical Society of Frederick County.*
Front cover, bottom: Middletown Valley vista. *Courtesy of the Carl Brown Collection, FCPL.*
Back cover, top to bottom: Burkittsville vista. *Photo by Davis Hall*; Evangelical Reformed Church, Trinity Chapel clock tower, City of Frederick. *Courtesy of the Historical Society of Frederick County*; War Correspondents Arch. *Photo by Davis Hall*; Utica Covered Bridge. *Courtesy of the Carl Brown Collection, FCPL*; Point of Rocks train station. *Photo by Ray S. Price.*

First published 2012

Manufactured in the United States

ISBN 978.1.60949.775.0

Library of Congress CIP data applied for.

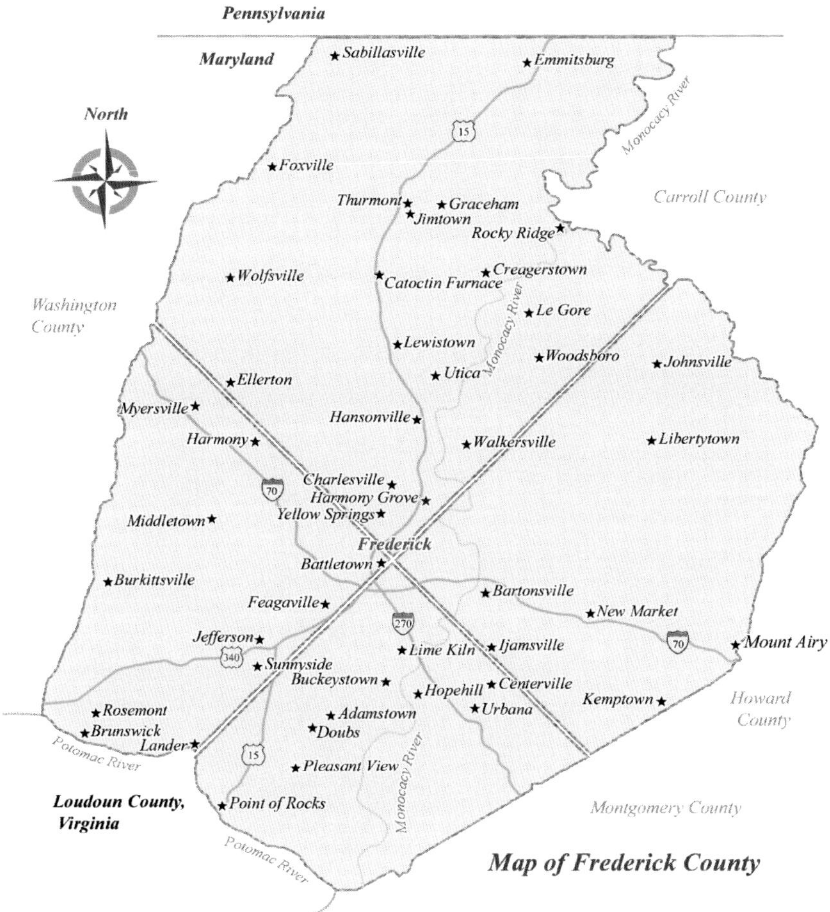

Map of Frederick County

Contents

Foreword

Nineteen sixty-seven was a crossroads for both me and Marie Erickson. This was the year of my birth, so I had my work cut out for me. As for Marie, challenge and transition came in moving to Frederick County, Maryland. She found herself in a place that had been a true crossroads from its founding in the 1740s, not only of transportation routes, but also of American history.

Separate roads led newcomers such as us to Frederick. I moved to Frederick at age seven from Delaware, but Marie came to this community in her mid-thirties, much more learned and experienced. Her arrival here shortly followed the Civil Rights movement, and she became captivated by existing reminders of Frederick's segregated past and what those meant for its future.

The *Crossroads* articles gave Marie a creative challenge and outlet for making sense of what had occurred here in terms of race, cultural relations, class, commerce and religion. Ironically, I met Marie in 1997 while researching and planning a television documentary inspired by my fascination with the cultural landscape of Frederick County. At age thirty, I was exploring the African American experience in this unique geographical setting between county borders of the Potomac River and Virginia to the south and the famed Mason-Dixon Line and Pennsylvania to the north.

As a young white male born after the civil rights movement, I was trying to truly understand and capture that story. Enter Marie Erickson.

I was repeatedly referred to Marie and was amazed to meet a white woman so interested and uniquely intertwined with the black population of our community. I immediately began reading her *Crossroads* articles and found that she had captured the essence of what I wanted to do with my project, and much more.

Marie's approach seemed to intersect a place, life, person or event in midstream, much the way roads intersect. She enjoyed telling a story in a non-chronological way, focusing on her subjects in the present setting while respecting their individual histories. Always feeding her own curiosity, she saw connections that many of us simply overlook.

Marie shared her research and interviews, making me aware of people and events happening around me. For example, in 1997, she introduced me to Arnold Delauter, then in his nineties, and Ardella Young, age one hundred. I was fixated on what each of these individuals had experienced earlier in life, especially in a segregated Frederick. I was also fascinated with the fragments of what remained of their ancestors' respective post-emancipation enclave homes of Pleasant View and Halltown.

Marie made me realize that the most important goal of each of her articles was conveying the current day presence of these people and places, not just their past. The locations are still evident; key landmarks still standing, individuals still living, each able to paint a picture of the past through the lens of the present day.

She was not afraid to take on tough subjects. She was a keen observer and an even better listener. Marie's cognitive retention for names, dates and minute details was phenomenal. She was a true conduit, able to connect people and information to bring out stories and facts long forgotten or incomplete. Marie Erickson was more than a friend; she was a mentor and teacher.

—Christopher Haugh

Documentary filmmaker, Scenic Byways and Special Projects Manager for the Tourism Council of Frederick County.

Acknowledgements

Compiling nearly fifty previously published articles, locating related photographs and revisiting the communities my mother profiled would not have been possible without many generous individuals and organizations. My heartfelt thanks to Mary Mannix, manager, and Carolyn Magura, associate, of the Maryland Room at the C. Burr Artz Public Library, Frederick County Public Libraries, who gave me access to the Carl Brown Collection and also provided valuable information for the bibliography. Heidi Campbell-Shoaf, executive director of the Historical Society of Frederick County, and Rebecca Crago, HSFC Research Center director, who provided historical images from the archives. Rebecca O'Leary, curator of the Brunswick Railroad Museum, who gave me access to the museum photo collection. John Kinnaird, who shared the spectacular Robert S. Kinnaird Collection of Historic Thurmont Images. Liz Scott Shatto, Historic Sites Consortium coordinator and Chris Haugh, scenic byways and special projects manager for the Tourism Council of Frederick County, who opened many doors. (Chris also found time to write the foreword.)

Thanks to Ray Price, my father, who provided twenty-year-old negatives of photographs he took while traveling the county with my mother on research expeditions. My sister Blyth McManus, who served as chief proofreader and cheerleader. Davis Hall, my husband and the best collaborator in the world, who created graphics, took photographs and made more trips to Frederick County than he imagined possible in one lifetime.

Thanks also to Hannah Cassilly, senior commissioning editor of The History Press, who saw the potential of these collected articles to delight and inform readers and guided me through the process of compiling them. All of these people gave freely of their time, knowledge and resources to make the dream of this book a reality.

Also worth noting is the Maryland State Archives, which provides Maryland Historical Trust surveys and National Register of Historic Places inventories online, enabling me to cross-reference photo captions; and the image collection of the Library of Congress. Thanks to Tom Gorsline, the former publisher of *Frederick* magazine, for suggesting in early 1990 that my mother visit a small Frederick County village to see what was there to write about, thus setting the whole series in motion.

As my mother wrote these articles, she truly enjoyed meeting the people whose stories brought personal elements to historic context. She deeply appreciated the contributions of Edna Albaugh Buhrman, Carl Brown, Ardella Young, Mildred Stine, Charles and Pauline Stup, Glenna Crutchley, Harold Shorb, Priscilla Rall Smith, Pauline Leatherman, Betty Willard, Jim Holton, Erin Dingle, Jerry Moser, Marlin LeGore, Charlie Green, Martin and Connie Odale, LeRoy Dinterman, Ron Bucher, Franklin and Marie Stambaugh, Mary Ellen Cummings, Paul Fry, Virginia Draper, Leah Spade, Bonnie Andrews, Jim Snively, Anna Belle Wickless, Richard D. Costlow, Margaret Ringer, Ed and Nancy Bodmer, Rowena Hildebrand, Arnold and Mary DeLauter, Marcella V. Snowden Thompson, Mary Lyles, Roger and Margaret (Lawson) Whalen, Bernard Brown, Jennie Weedon Lee, Bessie Lee Brown, Grace Grove Sappington, Bill Brosius, Virginia Brosius Thomas, Royal Lawson, David Young, Cornelia Hickman, Mary Herber, Conard Hawker, Eurath Ann Selckmann, Ethel Loeb, Drs. Martha and Gerald Schipper, Martin Schipper, Alice Hill, Sally Thomas, Nelson "Bing" Myers, Barbara Norris, Cliff Falcon, Marianne Browning, Maxine Browning, Pastor Laura Easton and David Easton, Ada Beale Poole, Travis Norwood, Margaret Routzan Miller, Julien Delphey, Oscar Baker, Herman Beck, Alverta Falconer, Frank Shaw, Paul Zimmerman, Margaret Kent, Gladys Brown Lee, Lord Nickens, George Hardy, Mary Margrabe, Anne-Lynn Gross, Sam Crone, James Feaga, Diana Droneberg Fox-Holter, Clarence Ford,

Gertilene Nichols, Louise Horman, Charles Smith, George Brigham, Bryan Hanes, Gil Stroup, Margaret Dutrow, Elizabeth Frye, Mary Ann Mauzy, Margaret Krone, Larry Hauver, Effie Hind Roderuck, Teresa Harris and Sayyd Abdul Al-Khabyyr.

Thanks most of all to my mother, Marie Anne Erickson.

—Ingrid Price

Introduction

This book is written by, and is a tribute to, my mother, the late Marie Anne Erickson.

Maryland—traversed over the years by roads, rails, canals and footpaths—has been a crossroads since Native Americans traded there in pre-Columbian times. Geographically equidistant from the northern- and southernmost of the original thirteen colonies, the state is crisscrossed with traces of industry, agriculture and travel among European settlers. Frederick County, situated in the west-central part of the state, bears the imprint of many generations of striving Americans.

The city of Frederick is truly a crossroads; located in the approximate center of its namesake county, it has long been the meeting point of major routes to the north, south, east and west. Now, Frederick's vibrant cultural scene and beautifully revitalized historic downtown make it attractive to tourists and residents alike. Its Visitor Center welcomes thousands of people every year. Like many who live in Frederick, my mother was fascinated by both its past and present.

But there is much more to Frederick County than the city at its core. Back in the early 1990s, *Frederick* magazine publisher Tom Gorsline was looking for fresh ways to explore and promote the many communities beyond the city limits. My mother's keen interest in history, her interviewing skills and lively writing style made her an excellent choice for the job. Her "Crossroads" series rapidly became one of the most popular features in the magazine, delighting readers who recognized their hometowns and encouraging newcomers and visitors to learn more about the area.

Battletown. Harmony. Pleasant View. The town names suggested fascinating stories, and my mother especially enjoyed seeking out the oldest residents in order to hear those stories firsthand. Floods and fires, sunlit picnics and moonlight sledding, the one-room schoolhouse and the church on the hill…these were all vividly remembered by people who had carried water by hand from wells in their youth, seen men walk on the moon in their middle years and were now encountering life in the computer age.

My mother wrote nearly fifty "Crossroads" articles from 1990 through 1995. (She even revisited a few towns for Frederick County's 250th anniversary in 1998.) Compiling them now, over twenty years after the first article was published, allowed me to walk in my mother's footsteps. Some landmarks have succumbed to time, some of the people originally interviewed are gone, but the excitement of discovery is as fresh now as it was then.

Because of her, on a recent sunny day I found myself perched on a burlap sack, flying down a nearly century-old giant wooden slide, laughing like a little kid. That morning, my husband and I stood by a cornfield, photographing a golden sunrise creeping over a white-steepled church in the distance while crickets sang. Later, we listened transfixed as a ninety-year-old living treasure told us stories of fires, floods and family in the parlor of her mountain home. The day before, we'd watched the mighty Potomac River sweep past the remains of the C&O canal, dodged huge rumbling trucks in a working lime plant and sifted through hundreds of historic photos in a museum archives. Caught up in the excitement of exploration, we understood what it was that kindled my mother's passion for these people and places.

If you'd ever met my mother in the street, she would have discovered a connection between you and Frederick County within minutes…because for her, all roads led here.

—Ingrid Price

North

Fire! Creagerstown Rises from the Rubble

It was the most beautiful day," recalls Mildred Stine, recounting what happened on June 2, 1914. "My dad was working for Mr. Hankey. The farmers used to help each other out." Though a small child at the time, Mrs. Stine vividly recollects seeing smoke and flames rising from Creagerstown that midmorning, as an accidental blaze rapidly spread out of control. Soon after the disaster, "a Shryock lady took my mother and me there in a wagon. The fire was a terrible thing. It was such a nice little town."

Harold Shorb, then six years old, describes the path the fire took: "See, it started from the creamery. When the man there made the fire in the morning, some sparks fell on the shingle roof and caught it on fire. It took the house next to it, then the next one and the town hall. It took another, and a store up on Blacks Mill Road." Mr. Shorb relates how the flames, fanned by strong winds, jumped the road and burned down the hotel and many more residences, until the north end of Creagerstown was gone. "Grandmother had brought cream to the creamery that morning. Around ten o'clock, it caught fire. There was no water, no fire engine, no nothing." He tells how the following day "my mother and grandmother brought me and my cousin, Lawrence Dorsey, to town in a wagon. We knowed a lot of people in town; they came to help folks out."

This is still an area where folks help one another out, where St. John's Lutheran Church (8619 Blacks Mill Road) holds an annual fundraising

The price on this old signboard reflects what fifty cents could buy in 1893. *Photo by Ray S. Price.*

dinner in the spring "for the cemetery upkeep and for the lights," Mrs. Stine mentions.

Other annual dinners benefit the church itself, on its present site since 1908. An eye-catching signboard displayed outside the parish hall on Thanksgiving Day advertised a real bargain—50¢ Full Dinner—only the sign was dated 1893! Held continuously since that date, with perhaps only a year or two missed, the meal could not be better, as the homemade fare is shared family style, and serving platters arrive hot and heaped to the tables throughout the event.

Coming by way of Pennsylvania, Germans settled Creagerstown district about 1750. Named after John Creager (spelled Kreiger originally), who laid out the town before the Revolutionary War, it is one of the oldest settlements in Frederick County. According to a newspaper description of September 5, 1922, "Creagerstown is pleasantly situated on the old Emmitsburg Road, 12 miles north of Frederick, one and a half miles from the Monocacy River and two miles from Loys Station on the Western Maryland Railroad. Strange to say, the village is four miles from Thurmont, four miles from Woodsboro, four from Rocky Ridge and four from Lewistown. One resident remarked, 'We are four miles from everywhere.'"

Located at what was formerly the junction of the Baltimore and Pittsburgh Roads with the Washington and Buffalo Roads (probably laid out on old Indian trails), it was an important point on the stagecoach route until the Frederick and Emmitsburg Railroads were built. At that time stood a tavern on each corner of the square. Jefferson Krise and C.L.

Valentine owned fine hotels in the village, until the 1914 fire destroyed them. Mr. Valentine rebuilt his Valley Hotel.

When the town hall was lost in the famous fire, a Creagerstown institution—its cornet band—also disappeared, as it was the place where the group rehearsed and held concerts. Mrs. Stine remembers that her father "belonged to the band, when I was a kid. They practiced every week. I'd go to my aunt's house, while my dad was at practice. There was lots of activity then. Or so it seemed to me, as a child."

Reminiscing about living first in the village's tollhouse, and then in the Stottlemyer residence close to Shryock's Mill, Mrs. Stine used to hear people say that the house was haunted. "I could hear things in the basement," she admits.

"The mill was the place where you got the news from the countryside all around. The farmers," she continues, "brought wagons of feed to be ground. They'd sit and wait. All the news came up." The mailman would ford Hunting Creek and also come to gossip.

"We walked across the mill races, going to school. There was a swinging bridge, too," adds Mrs. Stine.

A recent arrival, moving to a farm not far from Creagerstown fifteen years ago, Priscilla Rall Smith comments, "I don't feel like a newcomer, not like an outsider at all. I've been made welcome by people going back generations. I feel like my roots are here." She points out that "everyone is fixing up property. There's pride here. The town doesn't have a gas station or a big business or a post office, but it does have a little store. I feel that this is a unique place and a real slice of life as it was 100 years ago."

—*January 1991*

A "Garden Spot," Walkersville Continues to Charm

Walkersville was a wonderful town," says ninety-year-old Edna Albaugh Burhman, who as a small child lived on a big farm outside the village, "near the colored cemetery, between Walkersville and Woodsboro. Walkersville had a milk plant, a blacksmith shop and lots of businesses. I went with Daddy when he took the milk down and had the horses shod at Tom Fox's blacksmith shop."

Mrs. Buhrman remembers being allowed to attend school, a walk of two miles away, when only five years old: "My sister walked to school alone and had to cross the railroad tracks. The tramps who rode the rails would get off at the siding and stay in an old, tumble-down house there. Grace was afraid of the tramps, so my father or a hired hand would take her to school if possible, but they couldn't in the real busy season. Grace would cry and she'd want *me* to come along. Mama explained to the teacher, and she let me come to school. I liked to hear the 'big scholars' read; I memorized a lot." Mrs. Buhrman says she never saw a tramp, though. "There weren't too many freights that came up on that road."

Scharf's *History of Western Maryland* lists a colored school in the Walkersville area, to which many youngsters, in far-flung locations, had to hike even farther than two miles. For the term ending in the spring of 1881, teacher Adelaide Chambers had forty-four pupils to instruct in her small schoolhouse of logs. Many of their parents, too, walked long distances to reach places of employment in Walkersville and Woodsboro.

The 1886 Frederick County directory describes Walkersville as being on the Frederick and Pennsylvania Line Railroad and on the Frederick and Woodsboro turnpike (Maryland Route 194), seven miles northeast of Frederick. At that time, the settlement had a lawyer, two ministers, three doctors, four stores of various kinds, a lumberyard, a post office and a newspaper just started by Augustus Clem—*The Walkersville Enterprise.* "Most pleasantly situated in the midst of Glade Valley," Walkersville was termed "the garden spot of Frederick County."

In 1977, the community published an eighty-fifth anniversary commemorative book to celebrate its 1892 incorporation as a town. *Walkersville, Maryland—The Tale of Two Villages* points out that "at one time Frederick County was one of the largest corn canning areas in the country, supporting 12 different factories. During the first half of this century, the Monocacy Valley Canning Company, seasonally employing many local people, operated in the village." Acreage planted in corn underwent a decline during the '40s, however, as more and more farmers turned to milk production. The cannery shut down in 1948.

The wholesale Glade Valley Bakery on Main Street opened its doors in 1917, serving Central Maryland; Loudoun County, Virginia; Jefferson County, West Virginia; and Adams County, Pennsylvania. Drivers proudly pose with their trucks in the mid-1920s. *Courtesy of Charles and Kathryn Nicodemus.*

A business approximately the same age as the one-hundred-year-old town continues to thrive. T.R. Saylor & Co. has been in the same location at 15 Main Street since 1907. Saylor's Hardware is still owned by the same family, and while the tinning and roofing part of the business is gone, hardware and household items of all description are offered for sale.

At the time of the town's incorporation, Dr. John Nicodemus was a landowner. Williams's *History of Frederick County, Maryland,* tells that he was a successful and well-known practitioner of the county and also "a staunch advocate and active supporter of the Prohibition cause."

Named after John Walker, who laid out the place in 1845, Walkersville is actually a combination of two villages, neither of which was platted. Georgetown is considered the older community. Scharf's history mentions that the village was named in honor of early settler George Cramer, and "it is on the Frederick and Pennsylvania Railroad, but the station is called by the railroad Walkersville."

The eighty-fifth anniversary book also notes, "The land on which Walkersville is now located traces its history to parts of three tracts, Monocacy Manor, Dulaney's Lott, and Spring Garden, established prior to the Revolution, and, subsequently, a single tract, called 'Federal,' resurveyed after the confiscation (from Loyalists) by the State, composed of portions of each of the three original tracts." Early settlers—mostly German and English—"found this an open, gently rolling area among the forests, and therefore called it 'The Glade.' The surrounding forests are gone, but the name remains with us."

Georgetown founder Cramer donated a lot on what is now Main Street for construction of "Georgetown Chapel," said to be the oldest church structure in the town in use, leased by St. Timothy Catholic Church.

An 1828 split among the local Methodists resulted in the formation of two congregations, Methodist Protestant and Methodist Episcopal. While they continued to worship in the same building for twenty-five years, the two congregations vied for control "by placing and replacing door locks until 'Providence interfered by wrecking the building,'" states the little commemorative book.

When the Methodist Episcopalians built a new meetinghouse in 1855 on the same site as the destroyed one, near Israel's Creek, they may have given this small house of worship one of the longest names ever applied to a church to confound the other group—Methodist Episcopal Church of the United States of America of the Israel's Creek Meeting House in Frederick County and the State of Maryland.

For many people, it was a racehorse that gave Walkersville a degree of fame. In 1939, Challedon, sired by Challenger, from the W.L. Brann farm near Walkersville, won California's prestigious Santa Anita Handicap. *The Tale of Two Villages* says of their home: "The Glade Valley Farm fields stretched over an area of 150 acres of beautiful and rolling land…The lake on the farm used to be the village ice pond from which residents of the town used to cut ice." Since the early '70s, Glade Towne development has occupied that attractive land.

Of present-day Walkersville with its many amenities, Mrs. Burhman observes, "It's grown up now, but it's still a wonderful place."

—April 1992, Walkersville Centennial

Snakes, Surveys and Sabillasville

Nestled in a high mountain valley, Sabillasville and environs appear peaceful and orderly. From time to time a century ago, however, deep-rooted feuds would surface, particularly during elections, and the Hauver District (named for people of German origin) was the site of many bloody encounters between the mountaineers—"Swissers"—and those who lived in the valley.

A Swiss-born gentleman named Peter Zollinger, no doubt attracted by the mountainous country, settled early in the district and owned the land on which Sabillasville was built. Located in northern Frederick County and originally called Zollinger's Town, the pretty village was renamed, after his death, in honor of his wife, Servilla. According to Scharf's history, she was "a lady held in affectionate remembrance by the whole community, but in the course of time the name became adulterated into 'Sabillasville.'"

Outside St. John's Reformed Church, at the crossroads of Sabillasville and Harbaugh Valley Roads, a plaque mounted on a stone honors the original settlers in Harbaugh Valley, 1760: George, Ludwig and Jacob Harbaugh, brothers who were natives of Switzerland. Paul Fry, who has spent most of his eighty-two years living in Sabillasville on sites overlooking Harbaugh farmland, isn't so sure that Harbaughs were the first settlers here, but his research has not uncovered an earlier name. What may have seemed a benevolent setting when Paul's family moved to the hamlet proved otherwise. They literally had to stay on their toes as they went about tending their property. "We killed forty-three copper snakes in the hog pen," explains Mr. Fry, "and one night we killed one in the kitchen."

A well-stocked store owned by David and Lewis Crawford and John Stern's comfortable hotel were busy here long ago. The presence of the Victor Cullen Center probably accounted for a good part of their business. Built about the turn of the century to treat people with tuberculosis, it remained a center of employment through the Depression and during World War II (when Sabillasville's population was around 220), according to Ron Bucher, volunteer coordinator for the facility, now a state-run home for the intellectually disabled. Mr. Bucher has heard that on evenings when TB patients were not in attendance, townspeople were invited to enjoy movies at the hospital's theater.

Paul Fry recalls being taken by "the welfare woman" to have Dr. V.F. Cullen take a look at him. "I was sixteen years old," Paul recounts, "and weighed ninety-six pounds." Dr. Cullen's diagnosis: "Give the boy something to eat!"

Mr. Fry remembers when the county designated $140,000 to build four schools, but when Sabillasville's turn came, only $18,000 remained for

Dramatic stone masonry characterizes the original Victor Cullen Center architecture. *Photo by Ray S. Price.*

construction. Located on Sabillasville Road and now housing a church is the four-room school built "about the time the banks closed—it took two men and four horses six days, for a sum of $30, to prepare the site," says Mr. Fry. But that's not the school he attended. Neither was the earlier schoolhouse on Harbaugh Valley Road, some years ago converted into a residence. Mr. Fry was instructed in the two-room school at Friend's Creek. Pupils through grade three were taught on one side, and the rest, through grade six, on the other. He relates, "There was people coming to school that was fully grown. They'd only come in off the farms when there was no work in the wintertime. In the sixth and seventh grades, we studied eleven or thirteen subjects," he comments, "but not every day. We had things like Nation and State, and Our Ancestors in Europe.

Manufactured by W. & L.E. Gurley, of Troy, New York, this antique surveyor's compass served Paul Fry well. *Photo by Ray S. Price.*

"For fifty years, George W. Monahan was schoolteacher here," Mr. Fry continues. "We all respected him. He taught me how to survey. I surveyed just about everything on those mountains that you can see from here, clear to Emmitsburg," he indicates with a gesture. "The regular surveyors couldn't find the corners—can't find 'em in the old lots." Long-ago farmers who owned wood lots on those forested mountains enjoyed additional income by supplying charcoal to the Catoctin Furnace smelters.

Pooles Hardware and Supply (using the slogan "Trustworthy Hardware") is now the only store in town. Although not owned by Pooles, it carries that name because Jim Poole and his brother used to run a blacksmith shop on that Sabillasville Road site.

If you should be of a mind to check out the quarry on Brown's Quarry Road, save yourself the trouble. Roscoe Brown, who was a county commissioner, did decide to open a quarry there, but Mr. Fry, who drove Mack trucks for Mr. Brown for thirty cents an hour when in his twenties, says, "He couldn't make a go of it."

The townspeople are friendly, and if you happen to drive up that way, be sure to wave to Paul Fry. You may even find him ready to chat on his porch for a bit—an experience guaranteed to alter the way one perceives old Zollinger's Town.

—July 1990

Charlesville: A Vanishing Village

Although it appears on maps, there are no signs telling travelers along Opossumtown Pike that they are now entering Charlesville. But you know you have reached that small community when you see the brick facade of Faith United Church of Christ, which sits prominently on a rise in the landscape. A house of worship has stood on that site since 1881, and the church's presence continues to enhance the peacefulness of this rural place.

Folks are not sure just how old Charlesville is, but according to *Pioneers of Old Monocacy*, about 250 years ago the midpoint for German settlers along the German Monocacy Road was located just outside nearby Bethel, on the route to Mountaindale. The names of some of the earliest settlers, reputed to be industrious and thrifty, can still be found today in the area, both on the old tombstones in Faith's graveyard and on the mailboxes of living descendants.

"Pleasantly situated seven and a half miles from Frederick, from which point a daily mail is received and dispatched, the place takes its name from Charles Broadrup, Esq., an enterprising, wealthy citizen, who owns most of the land in the village and several fine farms in the neighborhood," states an 1886 directory of Frederick County.

Lifelong Charlesville resident Charles Stup, seventy-three, recalls that the farms were grants amounting to about 1,100 acres. "When children married, 50 acres would then go off to each one," he explains, adding that the Stups' farm traces back to the Ramsburg family.

Between 1882 and 1901, inhabitants of the village could pick up mail at their own little post office in the corner of Charles Broadrup's store. Anna Zimmerman, Charles Stup's great-grandmother, served as postmaster and also minded the store. "On Saturday nights at the store my grandfather cut hair," Stup recalls. "It cost a nickel a head, and he kept the money in a cigar box. We still have that cigar box upstairs."

Parker Stull kept a store in Charlesville for eighteen years. He carried feed for the steers and chickens that populated the farms, making deliveries from his spring wagon pulled by a horse named Alice, according to Stup.

In addition to Faith Church, visitors to the community can still see the buildings that housed both the general store-post office and the red-painted blacksmith shop. They stand near the bridge spanning Tuscarora Creek at the intersection of Opossumtown Pike and Sundays Lane. But the community hall, where people would enjoy concerts by such favorite groups as the Yellow Springs Band, is gone. Charles Broadrup's gristmill has disappeared too, yet the creek continues to pass picturesquely through the village.

At one time, neighboring Bethel was considered a central point for the communities of Charlesville, Mountaindale, Yellow Springs and Hansonville. Indeed, the families and histories of Charlesville and Bethel are closely intertwined.

Charlesville youngsters would bike a mile down the pike to Bloomfield School. It continued to operate until the consolidation of county schools in 1934. The school's last teacher, Glenn M. Pryor, still resides at White Rock.

School was open even when the snow was higher than the fences, but the winter weather was not without its advantages. "They didn't cinder the roads then, and eighteen or twenty kids would go sledding on the hill, where they'd pack it down," Stup says. "You'd go down the road and clear across the bridge."

Later, when he was twenty years old, Stup would help others shovel out Opossumtown Pike down to Poole Jones Road—a distance of more than two miles—in the days before county road crews existed. "You'd be surprised at how fast it would go," he says. Then the volunteers trudged on into Frederick for groceries at Weddle's Store. Unfortunately, if the wind blew all night, the road would be closed in again.

Another link to the surrounding area was the trolley line between Frederick and Thurmont, with the trolley traveling through Bethel. In the early 1940s, during World War II, the trolleys stopped running, their tracks torn up and sold for scrap iron. With them vanished the vitality of this little community.

—*December 1993*

The "Land of Promise" Lies in Ellerton

Today, the tiny settlement of Ellerton is a quiet place, offering little indication of the bustling, self-sufficient crossroads community it used to be. "People didn't go into town like they do now," says Pauline Leatherman, lifelong resident of this northwestern Frederick County village, tucked between Myersville and Wolfsville. For forty years, Mrs. Leatherman and her husband, Arthur, have owned what was formerly the Bittle store. "I grew up in that store," she remarks, recalling how, as a next-door neighbor, she spent much of her childhood there. "Ellerton had two stores going at the same time—Bittle's and Summers's stores."

It's easy to spot the building that was once Bittle's, because between it and the road rests an imposing mechanical engine. "It was my dad's when he had a sawmill," explains Mrs. Leatherman. "That engine was in four states. You had to haul that one." She identifies it as a Frick. It now belongs to her son Harold, who runs the one business remaining near the intersection of Maryland Route 17 and Harp Hill Road, at the creek—a lawnmower and tractor repair shop. Other business establishments that thrived in Ellerton's past included a blacksmith shop, shoe store, creamery, cider mill and an undertaker.

Agriculture remains an important occupation around the community, and many of today's farming family names appeared early in this area's history. According to the 1886 Frederick County directory, fifty-two farmers received their daily mail in the late 1800s at the Ellerton Post

Office. Thomas F. Bittle served as the town's last postmaster when the office closed its doors in November 1901. The directory touted the hamlet, located thirteen miles from Frederick and nine miles from Smithsburg, in Washington County, as a healthy place to live, "with plenty of pure water, land is clay and dark loam, sells at from $40 to $75 per acre, produces fine quality of wheat, corn and potatoes; church and schoolhouse near the village; population about 100." Mrs. Leatherman estimates the present population as "no more than twenty-five, depending on how far out you want to go." That's even fewer than the forty-one pupils attending Ellerton School seventy-five years ago.

People had to work hard, and children performed their share of chores. "Dad came off the sawmill at night," recalls Mrs. Leatherman. "He also worked in the fall at the cider and apple butter plant in Smithsburg. He'd get up, milk the cows and move them over to the other side of the creek. I'd get the cows over in the evening and milk them before Dad came home." Folks made butter and cream; the hogs got the milk.

"This place was a garden," she continues, indicating the land around her home. "They grew potatoes and beans. There was just a patch of grass on either side of the house."

Martin and Rose's book, *The History of Wolfsville & The Catoctin District*, tells of an auto dealership that flourished in Ellerton through the '20s: "Wilbur Summers sold Star and Whippet cars from 1922 until 1927 when he moved his business to Myersville. He was a good salesman, and one year sold 40 cars in one day at the county fair, and won a prize. People used to take a Model T and a Star or a Whippet and chain them back-to-back to see which one had the best clutch."

Flowing through Ellerton under the little bridge on Route 17 is Middle Creek, a branch of Catoctin Creek, earlier called Abraham's Creek. While it enhances the picturesque quality of the rural scene, Mrs. Leatherman retains vivid childhood memories of it flooding. "I saw the creek coming up many a time," she says. "I was at Bittle's store during the big flood when a large woodshed washed away, and buildings and cattle were found clear down around Middletown. I saw a lot of that stuff come down. It hit the bridge and split like kindling wood." *The History of Carrollton Manor*, by William J. Grove, reports that "several flour mills stood between Ellerton and Wolfsville," and a powder mill operated there as well. Upstream from the village stood a covered bridge, which was apparently removed during the 1930s. A half-mile downstream a well-known gristmill and sawmill owned by Daniel Schweigert—Shady Grove Mills—operated until about 1920.

Swiss and Germans settled the Ellerton area in the 1750s; they were followed by a few English. Elder Daniel Leatherman, founder of all the German Baptist churches, lived on a tract called "German Plains." Another prominent person was Daniel Gaver, who donated the site for St. John's Church on Church Hill; his property was on the "Land of Promise" tract.

—*January 1993*

Got Goldfish? Lewistown Cornered the Market

Folks around here still talk about the winter of '32. During a terrible blizzard, in the depths of the Great Depression, a number of travelers on the highway found themselves stranded. Seeking shelter, they made their way to the "Chapel on the Hill"—and broke the church's doors in an effort to gain entry and survive the night.

It was not the first time this historic brick structure, a tourist attraction today, saved lives, for during the Civil War it served as a hospital. Prominent on the landscape, it is easily recognized as one approaches the town. From its founding in 1833, not long after Lewistown was laid out by Daniel Fundenburg and named after his son Lewis, this former "Methodist Episcopal" church, possessing a bell that could be heard down in the hollow, has played an important part in community life.

In those pre-electricity days when population was sparse, people coming to evening services—or perhaps a special event such as a revival—would carry along lanterns to illuminate their return in the dark after worship. The hills must truly have been alive with the sound of music, because it was customary for parishioners to lift their voices in hymn-singing as they followed the pathway home.

Attracted by rich farmland and beautiful countryside, not unlike the country they'd left behind, many who originally settled in the area around 1745 were Germans, some arriving by way of Pennsylvania. *The History of Frederick County, Maryland* describes Lewistown as a "fine

One can find in the cemetery's oldest part the names of Lewistown's earliest settlers. *Photo by Ray S. Price.*

village…on the Frederick and Emmitsburg road…At the close of the revolution a number of the Hessian prisoners who were quartered at Frederick became American citizens and settled down in this district."

In the 1800s, Lewistown was a stagecoach stop and featured an inn where tired and dusty travelers could restore themselves with a hot meal before continuing their journey. Still standing, and occupied, on Hessong Bridge Road (Route 806) on the crest of the hill, this house faces across the street another building of interest—the former dwelling of E.D. Neighbours, the only medical doctor the little community has ever had. According to lifelong Lewistown resident Charlie Green, "He used all the land around the house at one time. It was a very attractive farm."

From the intersection of Lewistown and Hessong Bridge Roads, where he was standing, Mr. Green was also delighted to point out the location of the great flour and grain mill, built in 1824 by John Brien. Three stories high and of oak wood, it had stood, within Mr. Green's memory, near Fishing Creek. At one time called the "blue stream," the creek supplied water to the mill as needed, via a three-thousand-foot-long canal with a lock. This canal, of course dug by hand, was three feet deep and four feet wide. The mill's location on the edge of the road provided easy access for horses and wagons to take on loads.

Another business geared to travelers used to thrive on the main street. Martin's Grocery, owned by Martin and Connie Odale, does a brisk trade and seems to be the place for friends and neighbors to chat. But according to Mr. Odale, at one time this little store, where penny candy is still offered, was the location of Mary's Inn; tourist cabins on the property accommodated motorists.

Another type of local transportation important to people and industry in bygone days was the Blue Ridge trolley, part of the H&F (Hagerstown and Frederick) Railroad. One survivor may be seen in storage near the intersection of Putman and Mountaindale Roads. It was on the trolleys that commercial breeders shipped out many a container of fancy fish, destined to adorn gardens all over the world. Lewistown District—with soil noted for rather poor drainage—has long been an ideal area for commercial fish ponds. While many have been filled in and are now farmed upon, Mr. Green reflects that Lewistown was once called the "goldfish capital of the world." He adds, "Tressler's had fancy goldfish, and he shipped a lot of them to foreign countries. In twenty-four hours, the fish from his ponds would be for sale in London."

H&F trolley cars also carried visitors to a well-known resort, the Lake View Hotel. Built by C.J. Ramsburg in 1908, both the hotel and skating rink burned down in an accidental fire that occurred when a candle fell into dry, decorative Spanish moss. A youngster was killed in that out-of-control blaze. Although a large house associated with the hotel remains on the land, the fine orchard is long gone.

So are the blacksmith shop, sawmill, tannery, woolen mill and other enterprises. Recalling that his granddad owned the dye house near John Cronise's woolen mill, established in 1830, also powered by water from the canal, he describes how "Grandfather had big rollers, eight to twelve feet long, to squeeze the dye out of the cloth."

Lewistown's legendary Indian fighters and most of its industry may be gone, but one surmises that the stream is cleaner, and not far from the center of Lewistown, the trout fishing's not bad. Folks there are friendly, and the little town is worth a few minutes' side trip off busy Route 15 the next time you're in the area.

—*April 1990*

A Wild Ride on the Dinky Ends in Emmitsburg

Silver Fancy seems a rather poetic—and perhaps pretentious—name for a tiny frontier settlement. When its population increased to seven families, people called the place Poplar Fields and then Carrollsburg. Samuel Emmit acquired over two thousand acres in the area originally chartered to the Carroll family and began to sell lots. To honor this fellow citizen and local landowner, townsfolk agreed on the name Emmitsburg.

Founded in 1757 mainly by English- and German-speaking immigrants, Emmitsburg was incorporated in 1825. Roads lead south to Frederick, north to Gettysburg and west to Hagerstown.

"Though the old town pump has gone, and the fountain was taken away because it obstructed traffic, the town maintains an air of the quiet sweetness of the old days, emphasized by the existence of a long stretch of old-fashioned two-story houses along Main Street.

"The older portion of the town is west of these, however...once the real center of the old German houses, all of which were swept away in a fire of many years ago." These words by Folger McKinsey, the "Bentztown bard," in a 1938 *Baltimore Sun* are pertinent today: earlier this year the quaint community with its federal architecture gained a listing on the National Register of Historic Places in recognition of its notable past.

While many people think of world-famous canonized "daughter" Elizabeth Ann Seton, born 1773, when they think of Emmitsburg, there was also a famous "son" named John Armstrong, born 1772.

A triptych souvenir postcard shows Mother Elizabeth Ann Seton, the Stone House, the White House free school and the Chapel Tomb where she is buried. *Courtesy of the Historical Society of Frederick County.*

His reputation as possibly America's finest antique gunsmith is known throughout the country.

According to Wade Chrismer, in the town's history compiled by Emile and Mary Nakhleh in 1976, residents of Emmitsburg had strong pro-South feelings during the Civil War. Townspeople warmly received Confederate troops in 1862; the South was at that time under the impression that Maryland was going to join its cause.

This book tells that in 1906 a priest who had been a prefect during the war wrote, "In and around the College…a very bitter feeling towards the North. Dr. McCaffrey in his remarks was exceedingly bitter." It evidently puzzled the writer as to how Dr. McCaffrey, then president of Mount St. Mary's College, "managed to get away with what he did without being arrested." It is noted that "though he claimed that it was in the interests of neutrality, Father McCaffrey refused to let the American flag be displayed on the campus when Lincoln was shot. Federal orders were issued for every house to display some sign of mourning. An official visited the college, but there was no sign visible, until Dr. McCaffrey produced a small piece of crepe on a door which had been opened back so that it would not be visible until disclosed."

At least 232 Sisters of Charity, however, from Emmitsburg served during the Civil War in many military hospitals—Richmond, New York, Philadelphia, Baltimore and Frederick included—and even on a number of battlefields, heroically trying to save the wounded of either side. Two were natives of Emmitsburg: Sister Mary Catherine Chrismer and Sister Mary Rosina Quinn.

A few readers may remember when "the Dinky" ran the nearly eight miles between Emmitsburg and Rocky Ridge. One of the smallest railroads in the country, organized in 1868 and dissolved in 1940, it was financed largely by the Sisters of Charity at St. Joseph College so students and visitors could avoid a time-consuming round-trip of sixteen miles by horse. It was said that "many new students got his or her first taste of Emmitsburg college life during a wild ride on 'the Dinky' in September."

According to the *News*, September 21, 1944, not everybody got the word when the rail line closed: "Mrs. James Tucker of Boston, Mass., en route here to place her daughter in St. Joseph's College, bought railway tickets in New York for Emmitsburg via the Emmitsburg Railroad. The mother and daughter arrived at Emmitsburg Junction at night to learn that the rails had been taken up some years ago, leaving them and their luggage stranded at the junction. Guy Baker, who operates the mail and express truck between the junction and Emmitsburg, gave them and the luggage a lift to the college."

—August 1992

Moravians Found Sanctuary in Graceham

For some people, the mention of Graceham probably evokes images of a white-stuccoed church—or millions of birds, a la Alfred Hitchcock. Recognized by most researchers as the site of the earliest Moravian church in Maryland, the village in northern Frederick County attracted national attention in the mid-1970s when hordes of unwelcome avian visitors inexplicably came to roost here. Starlings were introduced into this country long after the Moravians' arrival from the Old World—but the settlers would have known the species in Europe.

But before the birds' unexpected invasion, Graceham's rural tranquility had been undisturbed except by the rumble and smoke of trains passing only a few yards from the cemetery in years gone by. "A station on the Western Maryland Railroad, 57 miles from Baltimore and 14 miles from Frederick, is delightfully situated in a healthy climate, with plenty of pure water," notes the 1886 *Frederick County Directory*. The community boasted good land producing a variety of crops, plus mail service, a church, public school, several stores and other enterprises.

About seventy-five years earlier, enough tradespeople, as well as a physician—all church members—thrived, making Graceham virtually self-sufficient.

"I used to hear wondrous reports of the town of Graceham," wrote Dr. Charles Hoffman, of Frederick, before the turn of the century. "My grandfather owned a farm in that vicinity, and members of the family visiting there brought back curious accounts of the inhabitants, their manners and customs, and especially of their religious life. They seemed to live apart from their neighbors in the world."

Later, Dr. Hoffman would visit the picturesque place himself and see "the Moravian church…on rising ground at the eastern end of the town." He found that "one of the most curious points of interest is the well-kept graveyard. The men are all buried on the right side from the entrance, and the women on the left. Immediately in the rear are the children's graves, and still farther back are those of strangers."

Most of the early settlers were of the Moravian faith. The Protestant Moravian Brethren, described as earnestly pious, originated in Moravia and Bohemia. Persecution and exile during and following the Thirty Year's War nearly caused them to die out, but in eighteenth-century Germany the sect experienced a revival, and members were permitted to build a village in Saxony. When England offered the group a tract of land in its North American colony of Georgia, Moravians began arriving in 1735. But by 1740, the colony, finding the Spanish inhabitants unfriendly toward Germans, headed for Pennsylvania. Soon after, they filtered south into Maryland.

At Graceham, worshiping began in people's homes about 1745. A full-fledged Moravian congregation arose in the little community, where it continues to flourish today. Reverend A.L. Oerter's 1913 history of the village notes the original German name for the flock was "Die Gemeine in Manakosy." The book also recounts how Bishop John de Watteville bestowed the present name on the congregation and community during an official visit to America's Moravian congregations in 1785. The bishop "expressed his earnest wish that Graceham might be a 'hamlet' in which the grace of God would abound."

Religion played an important role in governing the lives of Graceham's residents. For example, the Congregation Council required farmers to keep their cows in a yard or stable on Sundays during cold weather because wandering livestock would devour the hay out of churchgoers' sleighs. People needed the herbage to warm their feet on the drive back home.

The church is about all that remains of the institutions and businesses from the past. Even the post office has disappeared. Jim Holton, who has lived in Graceham for twenty years, says everyone looks down Route

77 to Thurmont for those things. "Graceham is really the perfect small town," Holton says. "It's a very close community, so it kind of polices and takes care of itself. Everyone draws together for weddings, births and funerals."

Holton speaks warmly and from first-hand experience about the helpfulness extended to a neighbor. "When I first moved here I wanted to do countrified things. I raised pigs to go to the butcher." But Jim found he had a problem when it came time to haul the animals to market. "I looked at the truck, and then at the pigs. How was I going to get them in?" When folks learned he needed a hand, they loaned him a bigger vehicle and helped him load it up. "That's the kind of community it is," he says.

—*August 1993*

Hidden from the Highway, Hansonville Holds Harper History

A quarter of a century ago, improvements to U.S. 15 bypassed tiny, unincorporated Hansonville. According to one longtime resident, "the bypass made it a little quieter. Tractor-trailers used to shake the house. Now wrecks (on U.S. 15) put traffic through here sometimes."

The community lies 5.5 miles north of Frederick and 2.5 miles from Harmony Grove, important to Hansonville at one time for its Frederick and Pennsylvania Line railroad station. Stagecoaches used to stop at the little settlement, and up until the turn of the century, travelers passing through town on the Emmitsburg turnpike were delayed as they paid a fee at the tollgate house. A log building beneath shingles, the 1.5-story tollhouse has been a private home for many years.

Edna Albaugh Buhrman's father and mother farmed what was then the Snook property in Hansonville at the time of Edna's birth in 1902, and her older sister attended school there. Edna was a baby when the family moved a few miles away, but the Albaughs continued to maintain close ties with folks in the friendly community.

According to Mrs. Buhrman, it was the kind of place where neighbors and friends would visit. She adds that "many of the people attended St. Paul's Lutheran Church in Utica." One family that occupied a prominent place in Hansonville's history was particularly talented musically: "The Harpers all played instruments and sang. They had beautiful voices. All of them were members of the church," she recalls.

The Harper Quartet was popular. Effie Harper Stottlemyer played organ in the church.

"They lived in the big house," says Mrs. Buhrman. "It had a beautiful front lawn, grass all the way down to the road." Once she attended a party there on a pleasant evening, when the King family owned the place. The yard was a lovely sight with many Japanese lanterns. "You can't see it today. It's all grown up in trees and bushes," Mrs. Buhrman adds.

It was Joshua and Matilda Miller Harper who built the red brick Harper house. The next people to live on the property were Richard Keller and Phoebe Craver Harper. Wealthy enough to own slaves, the Harpers freed them when the Emancipation Proclamation took effect. While some former slaves left to begin a new life elsewhere, others chose to stay on with the family, in familiar surroundings.

The Civil War touched Hansonville only slightly. One story relates that soldiers making their way to Gettysburg on a warm day paused at the home of Vernon and Libby Stull to ask for a drink of water. Old-timers remember hearing how the Stulls' large, pleasant living room provided the setting for many a lively party, when the family would move the furniture out and let the community's young people hold dances there.

Hansonville Road resident Mrs. Glenna Crutchley, whose grandmother was born a Harper, once asked her father, Glenn Stull, a respected schoolteacher and farmer, how the town got its name. He told her it was named after John Hanson. This illustrious citizen, who became president of the United States in Congress Assembled, came to Frederick County from Carroll County.

The town's post office long ago disappeared, but the old schoolhouse remains as a private residence. The former blacksmith shop is a garage. Remodeling has altered and preserved a number of original buildings here, some of which, like the tollhouse, were made of logs.

When asked what could be considered the boundaries of Hansonville nowadays, one person who lives on Hansonville Road replied, "Maybe from the White Cottage Inn to the Highway Exxon on the top of the hill." Although the tavern that once operated near the (now closed) White Cottage Inn went out of business a long time ago, Cactus Flats and the Airport Inn today offer refreshments on Hansonville Road. "They might consider themselves part of Hansonville. I don't know," the resident concluded.

The Shoemaker Grocery was a gathering place for local men, who sat by the potbellied stove and played checkers. Evelyn Shoemaker Stull posed in front in the late 1920s. *Courtesy of Glenna Crutchley.*

The quiet location, with easy access to a major highway, seems to suit those who have chosen to reside in the rural community. Mrs. Crutchley is delighted to be where her roots are and says, "I never want to leave Hansonville. I love it here."

—*January 1992*

Harmony Grove: "Just Say It's Paradise"

"Just say it's paradise, and that'll cover it all," says longtime Harmony Grove resident and author Carl Brown. Scharf's History of Western Maryland describes the community as it was over a century ago: "Harmony Grove, a pretty hamlet, is situated on the Frederick and Pennsylvania Line Railroad, two and a half miles from Frederick. It has a Methodist Protestant Church and a public school. N.R. Plummer is postmaster, and keeps a grain store, etc. J.C. Cronise, Thomas Miller, Abraham Trimmer, and W.J. Worman are millers; J. Metcalfe, millwright; and H.C. Grabenhorst, dairyman." By 1895, a cigar maker had also moved into the "pretty hamlet."

More than two hundred years ago, William J. Worman settled on 110 acres in Harmony Grove, and in 1886, Mrs. Mary Worman owned 375 acres there. Some of her stories have been handed down, and a favorite comes from the Civil War period. During that struggle, troops from both sides occupied the Worman family home. It seems that when those from the North headed for Gettysburg after an overnight stay, they took along the farm's livestock, leaving only one cow and one horse, without offering to pay. When confederates arrived, Mrs. Worman had a black hired man hide the remaining beasts in the woods. The soldiers did not discover the animals, but they determined that the farmhand could play the fiddle—and kept the poor fellow at it until late into the night. An exasperated Mrs. Worman put in an appearance downstairs and asked to speak with the

Harmony Grove's schoolhouse, built in 1876 and closed in 1910, later served as a private residence. *Courtesy of the Carl Brown Collection, FCPL.*

officer in charge. According to Carl Brown's book, *Harmony Grove*, "She told him that although there was a war going on they still had to tend the farm and they needed their rest. The officer said he was sorry and told the men that the entertainment was over."

In 1872–73, the Frederick Pennsylvania Line Railroad came through. Scott Worman watched the construction and remarked that excavation was done by hand, largely by Italian workers using two-wheeled carts and mules to haul away the earth. At one time, ten trains a day, traveling between Pennsylvania and Frederick, stopped at Harmony Grove.

The railroad replaced the bridge spanning the Monocacy River in the early 1900s. The company contracted with Mrs. Witter, who lived on a farm at Harmony Grove's north end, to perform what must have been the Herculean task of feeding the twenty or thirty workmen three full meals a day. Crude sleeping accommodations were set up in the barn.

Passenger trains continued to pass through the village until August 1948. But after the flood caused by Hurricane Agnes in 1972, the old bridge was left unusable. Brown's history reports: "The water came up to the first floor of the Clemson and Smith home at Route 26 and 355." The last freight train ran through the village on June 21, 1972. A trolley car system may someday operate on that roadbed to connect Frederick and Walkersville.

The widening of U.S. 15 in the 1950s had considerable impact on Harmony Grove. So much land was lost to the project by the Dutrow family, purchasers of the thirty-two-acre Cronise farm in 1916, that they sold the remainder in 1959 and resettled in Carroll County.

Mr. Brown recalls that the state tore down the Ramsburg Feed Warehouse and the Ramsburg home, with store and post office and railroad station, to connect old and new U.S. 15. "They used to have weekly produce auctions there of apples, oranges, bananas, celery," he remembers. "The Ramsburgs did a thriving business. Like all village stores, this was a gathering place for the men of the community."

Israel Delauter opened and operated a store at Harmony Grove's south end for a time.

George Houck built and lived in the first and most costly house in Harmony Grove. Several generations of the Bowers family subsequently owned or occupied the property and called it the "Pines"; in 1980, Mr. and Mrs. Ray Compton bought it and converted this large brick building on the east side of Wormans Mill Road into a bed-and-breakfast—Spring Bank.

Other structures in the community have been adaptively reused. Harmony Grove School closed in 1910, and Mr. and Mrs. T.B. Haywood eventually purchased the place and turned it into the Brocton Orchard tearoom. The orchard, from which the establishment took its name, was famous for fine fruit; most of its apples went to England, beginning their journey at the Harmony Grove railroad siding.

A *News-Post* article of August 10, 1926, describes the restaurant's outstanding location: "Ample space for parking automobiles has been provided, and the large lawn which commands a very picturesque view of the Catoctin mountain from Braddock Heights to Catoctin Furnace is arranged with tables and chairs for the accommodation of patrons." But the tearoom may have been too "swanky" and ahead

The grand Houck house, built in 1880, grew even larger in 1926 when young architect Charles Bowers designed a two-story addition. *Courtesy of Ray and Beverly Compton.*

of its time, for it operated only briefly. Brocton Orchard then used the building for storage, until Carl and Evelyn Brown bought and remodeled it into a residence.

In contrast, the 1878 Community Chapel stands in a sorry state. Erected on land donated by Isaac Cronise when dissension arose among members of the village's Methodist Protestant Church, and twice restored, it has been in disrepair after extensive damage by a young vandal.

Carl Brown has witnessed a number of changes during his fifty-year residency in Harmony Grove: "There were nine houses when I moved out there, and now there's nine and a half. It's growing to beat the band!" He adds that "it's the best place in the world to live."

—*June 1991*

Jimtown Owes Its Name to...a Bartender?

Few towns can claim the distinction of being named after a bartender. Jimtown, Maryland, a small community in northern Frederick County, received its plain name in the late 1800s when a problem arose over the number of feet between Jim Crouse's tavern and the local schoolhouse.

The distance between the two distinctly different buildings was not acceptable by government standards, and the tiny settlement was termed "country" and not an official town. Residents quickly turned the area into a town by choosing a name and erecting roadside signs proving the town's status. Now they could have a school.

Well-known citizen Crouse was chosen to be honored and remembered in "Jimtown." Elimination of the "country" designation satisfied the county commissioners and put an end to the controversy. The building in question, now a private residence, can still be seen on Moser Road.

The small yellow building that housed Crouse's Tavern dates back to 1877. The tavern was very popular due to the proximity of the village's crossroads and served as the "watering hole" for much of the area. Many of Crouse's customers would travel the mile from Thurmont to Jimtown to purchase liquor, since Thurmont was "dry."

Jim Crouse's establishment also served as a favorite place for gossip and information, especially since the tavernkeeper doubled as postmaster just before the turn of the century. Between 1910 and 1960, Crouse's

Tavern welcomed a different clientele, for Dr. George C. Zinkhan Sr. maintained a veterinary practice in the structure. Son George Jr., a farmer affectionately known as "Doc," now owns all four corners at Jimtown's intersection.

The Moser family has called the area home for generations. "There were a lot of turkeys here at one time," says eighty-three-year-old Jerry Moser, indicating the land that was once a turkey farm around his house with a wave of his hand. Moser points to traces of an old wagon road on his property as the likely location of the German Monocacy Road, the route taken by many German immigrants who settled in the area. "The road curved around and went to Catoctin Furnace," says Moser. "You can see it very plainly."

Authors Tracey and Dern state in their book *Pioneers of Old Monocacy* that "the German Monocacy Road continued its way west through Graceham, then south through Jimtown Crossroads, Lewistown, Bethel, and on to today's junction of Butterfly Lane and Mount Phillip Road."

Historians and church folks around Jimtown continue to speculate about the site of the old Monocacy (Monocasie) Church, which dated well back into the 1700s. Millard Milburn Rice, in his *New Facts and Old Families* (1976) found evidence "that the actual location was south of today's Thurmont, somewhere between the Jimtown Crossroads intersection of Moser Road, Jimtown Road (Maryland Route #550) and Hessong Bridge Road."

A small graveyard on Jerry Moser's property might have yielded some answers to the church's whereabouts, but unfortunately all but one of the eight headstones there were crushed early in this century during the upgrading of Moser Road (then Old Hagerstown Pike). Substantial fences of native stone also disappeared with the pulverizing equipment. The only remaining marker names John Hankey, who died in 1775.

Development has come to Jimtown in the form of Maple Run, an eighteen-hole golf course created by transforming two Moser farms in a cooperative family effort.

—October 1995

131 Years of Ore to Iron: How Catoctin Furnace Earned Its Keep

People always spoke of it as the "furnace"; I heard my father and grandfather speak of it that way," says Mrs. Edna Burhman, a Frederick County resident with a passion for history. "After the Revolutionary War, Hessian soldiers who wanted to stay in this country went to Catoctin Furnace. It was the Hessians who helped build those little houses. They're one-story, with an attic. People have been rebuilding them.

"A lot of the furnace operation was on the other side of the pike," she continues. "The railroad went through. The trolley line crossed right between the furnacemaster's [ironmaster's] house and the other works. I've crossed there many times."

W.J. Grove's History of Carrollton Manor recounts: "Iron ore was discovered at the base of the Catoctin Mountains and a furnace erected at what is now known as Catoctin Furnace. The iron made there was transported in boats down the Monocacy and Potomac Rivers. This furnace supplied iron in large quantities for domestic and other purposes."

According to an article in the *News* of March 30, 1924, it was actually "trusted Negroes owned by Launcelot Jacques" who conveyed the manufactured pig iron down the Monocacy River on flatboats. Slaves were an important part of the workforce keeping the furnace operating at peak efficiency. A decade or so ago, the Smithsonian Institution conducted an archaeological excavation at Catoctin Furnace's slave

First fired up in 1774, the furnace produced iron almost continuously until 1905. *The Robert S. Kinnaird Collection of Historic Thurmont Photographs.*

cemetery, as well as twelve other sites that were to be altered forever by the dualization of U.S. Route 15.

Thomas Johnson, a lawyer who became Maryland's first governor, and Launcelot Jacques, also a lawyer and a French Huguenot who took refuge in America, were business partners in a number of ventures. As their intention was mainly to develop Frederick County by establishing iron furnaces, they selected mineral-rich land as smelting sites. It was in 1769 that Baker Johnson, one of the Johnson brothers—including also Thomas, James and Roger—bought, dismantled and reconstructed the Hampton Furnace, which had been located in what is now Bruceville, on a site a few miles south of Mechanicstown, now called Thurmont. Not by chance did the furnace at Catoctin swing into operation in 1774, under the direction of ironmaster Roger Johnson, shortly before the Revolutionary War. Through the influence of Thomas Johnson, many federal and state government contracts for armament and ammunition were filled there.

In 1776 Jacques and Johnson dissolved their business association, with the former receiving as his share of the property the Green Spring Furnace estate (Richlands) in Frederick County.

It was Thomas Johnson who in the mid-1700s built Catoctin Manor as the ironmaster's residence; unfortunately, no preservation efforts materialized on its behalf, and the place stands in ruins. The property's fine boxwood hedge, however, was saved by being transplanted. The shrubs went to Washington, D.C., to grace the gardens of the White House and the Lincoln Memorial.

An excellent example of an early industrial village, Catoctin Furnace had in the area the materials necessary for iron production: limestone, used as a flux in smelting the iron; charcoal, from the forests nearby; and ore. All the facilities were there to convert iron ore into finished products. It was the only such site in Maryland.

Pots, kettles and Dutch ovens were manufactured there, as well as wagon wheels and construction material. For George Washington's Continental army, cannon and cannonballs were produced. Some of the machinery for John Rumsey's steamboat, the first steam-powered vessel tested in American waters, came from the ironworks at Catoctin Furnace. During the Civil War, it turned out iron plates for the Union warship *Monitor*.

Mildred Stine's parents enjoyed taking pictures of the little industrial settlement, "My daddy told me about the people working up at 'the furnace,' and another rough place was LeGore's Lime. A band of men would go from there to 'the furnace' sometimes and pick fights.

"There were a couple of stores there," recalls Mrs. Stine, a lifelong resident of nearby Creagerstown. "One day my daughter went with my aunt to the mill to buy flour. This was Kelly's Mill. If you'd buy a sack, you'd get a bowl. My aunt bought the flour, got the bowl, and gave it to Phyllis. There must have been a number of them given away," says Mrs. Stine, lifting out of a kitchen cabinet the one her daughter had so long ago received.

The last year the famous iron furnace was used—1905—also witnessed a great tragedy, when, according to a newspaper account, "27 Catoctin residents were killed and a large number wounded in the famous Western Maryland Railroad wreck of that year. Those killed were railroad employees." Nearly every family suffered a loss.

The site of Catoctin Furnace is part of Cunningham Falls State Park. Catoctin Mountain Park, northwest of Catoctin Furnace, has an exhibit on charcoal making.

The "great wall" at "the furnace" is still evident; the mortarless stone structure originally stood about 35 feet high and extended approximately 250 feet.

Not far from the furnace stands the stone church (Catoctin Episcopal Parish), long known as Harriet Chapel in honor of Harriet Brien, completed by John Brien in early 1828. It has been cared for and added on to over the years.

Catoctin Furnace Historical Society opens the Collier Log House, listed in the National Register of Historic Places, on weekends during the summer.

—*March 1991*

Ingenuity Sparks Industry in Thurmont

Nestled beneath the Catoctin Mountains, Thurmont has as close neighbors a variety of wildlife, an abundance of flowing water, spectacular greenery—and camps and presidents. When the federal government established the Catoctin Recreational Demonstration Area in 1936, it set in motion events that have provided this "gateway to the mountains" with presidential visitors from time to time. In an unique experiment, the Department of the Interior acquired fifty private properties to demonstrate that a park could be created from nearly worthless land, overcut for charcoal making, tanning and logging and worn out by poor farming methods. Later becoming Catoctin Mountain Park, this preserve attracted the attention of Franklin Roosevelt, the first president to maintain a getaway—Shangri-La—there. Called Camp David since Dwight Eisenhower renamed the retreat after his grandson, "Camp #3 Hi-Catoctin" continues to be the place, easily reached by helicopter or car, where residents of the White House and their guests come for rest and relaxation.

By a quirk of fate, there's a bit of Thurmont in the presidential home in Washington, D.C. When the Stoner house, at 15 East Main Street, was about to be razed in 1961, a young lay preacher with a deep interest in antiques learned of the scheduled sale of furniture from the property. There, Peter Hill chanced to see the still magnificent "Scenic America" wallpaper that had graced the front hall of the home for almost 125 years, the selection of well-to-do tanner William P. Jones. Hill negotiated with Mrs. Stoner and the wrecking crew foreman for permission to pry off and save the French-designed and made wall covering. For fifty dollars and in just three days' time, he claimed this forty-eight-foot-long composite panorama.

Hill's friend John Newton Pearce, of the Cultural Historical Section at the Smithsonian, suggested that his wife, who happened to be the White House curator, take a look at the unusual find. First Lady Jacqueline Kennedy, with some of her friends, also inspected the historic wallpaper. She admired the scenes and wished to use them in the executive mansion. Along with an needed additional twenty-five feet from a New York City antique shop, the panels went up on the walls of the White House's diplomatic reception room.

The National Society of Interior Designers paid Hill $12,500. Although $17,500 had been the agreed-upon figure, Hill graciously donated $5,000 in the name of Thurmont's citizenry.

Through the generosity of Baltimore philanthropists Lillie and Aaron Straus, two summer facilities for Jewish children—Camp Louise and Camp Airy—came to the Catoctin Mountains in the early 1920s. Miss Hannah Hammond, a black employee at Camp Airy, was familiar to generations of young campers and well known to the Thurmont community. She remains a part of it, buried upon her death in 1977 in what is now the United Methodist cemetery, predominantly white, by the Hammond family from Virginia, for whom she had worked most of her life. Retired Thurmont librarian Margaret Krone tells that she "would take Hannah to services at Harriet Chapel, where she always sat in the chair next to the organ. One day," recalls Krone, "Secret Service men were there; an agent was in her chair. Hannah told him, 'Young man, that's my seat!' He moved."

Industrial activities predominated in the village in its early days—hence the original name Mechanicstown, in use until 1894. Founder Jacob Weller and other German immigrants sought to settle in surroundings reminiscent of their homeland, and with the elements necessary for their trades, such as blacksmith, tanner, miller, cabinetmaker and wheelwright.

Weller's grandsons, Joseph and namesake Jacob, were impressed with a French import they purchased in Frederick—paper matches. Conducting experiments of their own, and, in the process, twice blowing up their

Miss Hannah Hammond of Camp Airy. *The Robert S. Kinnaird Collection of Historic Thurmont Photographs.*

own workshop, the brothers succeeded in 1825 in manufacturing the first friction match in America. Since they did not, however, patent their product, competing companies began to make "lucifer" matches as well, and the price plummeted. On the corner of Altamont Avenue and West Main Street, the Weller home—the "Match House"—still stands, with a second floor added sometime before 1900.

In an interview several years ago with local history buff Edna Buhrman, she revealed the existence in the early 1920s of a swindle in Thurmont: at the Annie-Laura Oil & Gas Company. Many citizens, convinced by a couple hustlers carrying bottles of oil supposedly obtained from some nearby boggy ground, invested in the enterprise. Buhrman recalls, "On July 6, 1921 my husband-to-be, R. Paul Buhrman, purchased ten shares of stock at one dollar each. I never saw any activity at the so-called

The only thing the Annie-Laura oil rig pumped out of Thurmont was money. *The Robert S. Kinnaird Collection of Historic Thurmont Photographs.*

Annie ·Laura Oil & Gas Company. Year by year the oil rig disappeared, as did the men who sold the shares of stock," Still in possession of her husband's certificate, Buhrman considers it a rare antique from Thurmont's past.

According to Thurmont Historical Society board member Erin Dingle, this organization, founded in 1987, has a "strong membership." It has been steadily involved in the restoration of the house at 11 North Church Street, donated to the society by Ethel Creeger eight years ago. One of the oldest homes in the community, two-storied with red brick over chestnut logs, it is open only by appointment for tours. Among the prized acquisitions is a walnut dresser, part of a bedroom set, bearing inside a drawer the label of an E.M. Smith, who was circa 1870 "manufacturer and dealer of furniture" and "undertaker in general. Mechanicsburg, Maryland." On Friday and Saturday, the Creeger House has limited library hours. The society also developed a walking tour of the town for elementary school children, with a descriptive brochure.

In a "History of Thurmont" prepared and read before the Historical Society of Frederick County in the early 1940s by Miss Linnie NcGuigan, she states that "the history of Thurmont will not be complete without mention of Amos T. Lucas, familiarly known as 'Tup,' who held the distinction for many years of being the only colored resident of the town." Indeed, his obituary in the newspaper of August 2, 1917, points out that "for at least 30 years he was the only colored person claiming residence in Mechanicsburg District, a thing few, and probably no other district in the state can boast of."

Born into slavery in Loudon County, Virginia, he was working for Dr. Henshaw of Lovettsville in the late 1860s, when the Henshaws moved to Maryland and brought Tup along. For more than forty years, he barbered in the Osler building, which stood at the corner of Church and W. Main Streets. In his *Catoctin Clarion* ads, he would lead with the phrase "The Art Tonsorial." Tup, like Hannah Hammond, is buried in the United Brethren, now United Methodist, cemetery in Thurmont.

For the 250th anniversary of Frederick County, the town plans to display a banner and issue a proclamation.

—February 1998, the year of Frederick County's 250th anniversary celebration

Sliding into Rocky Ridge

The 1886 *Frederick County Directory* places Rocky Ridge fifty-one miles from Baltimore, sixteen miles from Frederick and seven miles from Emmitsburg. That location has not changed, but land in Rocky Ridge no longer sells for the directory-listed century-old price of forty to sixty dollars per acre. Now, as then, however, "the crops of wheat, corn, rye, etc. are generally fine." The 1886 population figure of fifty has increased many times over. "Red slate and well-improved" still correctly describes the soil of Rocky Ridge, and the community itself is among the tidiest and prettiest in Frederick County.

Even residents knowledgeable about their local history are reluctant to assign a specific year as the village's date of founding. Research seems to indicate that the farm known as "Swan's Harbour" and owned by Franklin and Marie Stambaugh dates back to at least 1752. Since 1924, these 132 acres of gently rolling land with a bluff overlooking the Monocacy River have been in Franklin's family. The original log home, concealed beneath improvements and additions, continues to be a part of their farmhouse.

No documentation indicates who gave the little town, situated on the ridge stretching from Frederick to a bit south of Gettysburg, its name. Perhaps those who plowed the land and were most familiar with the area's ground-level ironstone shale formations simply began referring to this "rocky ridge"; shale outcroppings can easily be seen at the old Western Maryland Railroad cut through the village.

A relative newcomer to Rocky Ridge expresses deep affection for the place but states matter-of-factly, "If you don't go to church, or you don't belong to the fire company, or you don't quilt, then you don't have anything to do here." Those who choose to participate in the local institutions will find no shortage of pleasant and cooperative activities. Many volunteers are needed each October, for example, to turn dozens of bushels of local apples into ninety gallons of fresh apple butter.

Townsfolk are proud of lovely Mount Tabor Park. LeRoy Dinterman recalls that "it was started in 1915 or 1916, with four acres. The park has nine acres now." Marie Stambaugh tells of the 1951 fire that destroyed the park's wooden sliding board, but a quick rebuilding guaranteed its ranking as the longest and steepest slide in the county.

The Mount Tabor Church—United Church of Christ and Lutheran—owns and maintains the shaded property and hosts the park's annual spring festival and fundraiser, which features an antique tractor pull. Mrs. Mary Ellen Cummings observes, "When we have any kind of activity in the park, everybody is there, either looking in the park, eating or helping."

Several businesses flourished in the past. LeRoy Dinterman remembers, "Compton's was the last store in Rocky Ridge. It's been gone a good long time." The building itself is there, however, adjacent to the parking lot of the oldest church in town, the Rocky Ridge Church of the Brethren, on Motter's Station Road.

The boardinghouses, which once sheltered overnight travelers from Baltimore who came to visit the park, are also homes to families.

In 1949, thanks to the interest and hard work of Charles Mumma, Rocky Ridge's own fire company was established, and in 1966, the present fire hall, a community focal point, was dedicated.

For a dozen years, a rather unusual industry flourished in the village: The C.M. Engler Cigar Box Factory used to stand on the site where the volunteer fire company's parking lot is now located. The company's motto proclaimed "Superior quality, best lumber, neatly finished." LeRoy Dinterman says, "They made the boxes here, shipped them to other places to put the cigars in." For many years, it was thought that no boxes from this turn-of-the-century enterprise had survived. But Mr. Dinterman recently came across a nice specimen in which Swadener's "Nickel Boom!" cigars had been packed.

LeRoy Dinterman displays the only known surviving example of an Englar cigar box, produced by the thousands in Rocky Ridge around 1900. *Photo by Ray S. Price.*

"We burned wagonloads of these things," says Franklin Stambaugh ruefully, referring to the old cigar boxes. "Engler got Pop to clean out that old shed. We took wagonloads home, broke 'em up, and burned 'em." Now they would be prized.

Rocky Ridge boasts a large industry today—the Baltimore Brick Company, which owns eight hundred acres and utilizes the plentiful Gettysburg shale found here. Mr. Stambaugh calls it "some of the best brick-making clay there is." In operation for around a quarter of a century, the Rocky Ridge Works, with sixty-five employees, turns out a phenomenal forty million bricks a year in thirty different colors. Many go out of state, and some go out of the country, as, for example, to Canada.

Richard Stambaugh carries on industry on a smaller scale in an outbuilding at Swan's Harbour, where he makes custom furniture, such as conference tables, beds and cabinets. Franklin says, with justifiable pride, that his son's quality products have gained many prominent customers, strictly by word of mouth.

Older people in the area reminisce about fishing and swimming in the Monocacy River when they were children. Kids played marbles and dodge ball, too. Occasionally, they would, in the words of Mr. Dinterman, run off from school to play hooky or get into a bit of mischief at the schoolhouse. He remembers that once in a while, "someone would untie the bell rope, which then dropped down through the hole. The teacher would pay a quarter to one of the kids to put it back up!"

Mrs. Cummings, a local quilter, describes their get-togethers to sew as "our therapy sessions, because if you have a headache, if you have problems, you come here and feel better right away." This quieter, in many ways old-fashioned, pace of life is readily perceived by the visitor, and one comes away from Rocky Ridge refreshed in spirit and energy.

—July 1991

A Chestnut Church Serves Foxville's Flock

It was the last two-room schoolhouse in Frederick County," says Betty Willard of the little stuccoed building not far from Camp David. Describing the Foxville school as a good place for a new teacher to start out in, Mrs. Willard quickly found she needed to understand more than the three R's to do a proper job. "The first year I was there," she recalls, "they had a coal-burning stove. I didn't know how to operate it. After a while, we got a furnace.

"All the children would walk to school. Many of their parents worked in Thurmont, and the kids would come to school early. One of the two teachers would be there at 7:00 a.m."

Nowadays, attracting a sizeable crowd of parents to PTA meetings at most schools is not easy. But attendance at evening functions was never a problem at Foxville. "The school was the main thing in the community. People came to PTA meetings whether they had a child in school or not. It was a social thing, and refreshments were served," tells Mrs. Willard.

She adds that she has never forgotten the generosity and many kindnesses shown her in the little community.

In 1961, one year after she went to Thurmont to teach (and where she has been ever since), consolidation occurred; Foxville's friendly elementary school became surplus property. And what must have been the Frederick County school system's most unusual collection of books found itself dispersed, with many volumes going onto library shelves elsewhere.

Mrs. Willard explains that because of Foxville School's proximity to both Camp David and President Eisenhower's farm at Gettysburg, the daughter of Ike's horse trainer was enrolled there. Perhaps the little girl's school seemed to Mrs. Eisenhower, as she cleaned out cupboards one day at the presidential retreat, a suitable place to contribute boxes of no-longer-needed books. Mrs. Willard remembers that "a sailor drove a station wagon, with the donated books, to the school. Some had the signature of David Eisenhower."

The Lutheran church owns the former school property. In 1963 or 1964, Mr. and Mrs. George Spates purchased the schoolhouse, adjacent to their property, and gave it to Mount Moriah Lutheran Church for community purposes.

According to the dates on this church, the site's original structure was erected in 1830, and rebuilding took place in 1877 and 1919. Built of local mountain stone, the edifice displays the same handsome hues of color as do many of the region's other buildings and stone walls bordering productive fields. Backbreaking labor must have been the lot of early settlers who penetrated the wilderness, as they felled timber and moved rocks in what was first called Brownsville, then renamed Foxville.

Mount Bethel United Methodist Church was founded in 1836. The original building was made of chestnut logs, and people may yet refer to this house of worship as "Chestnut Bethel" church, though the log structure disappeared ninety years ago. An unusual and welcome feature in the present-day church is the sloping floor of the sanctuary, affording even those parishioners in the back rows a good view of the service.

Tombstones in the adjacent cemetery indicate that some of the earliest settlers in the area rest there. Through the efforts of Vernon M. Buhrman, the remains of John Poorman (an English language version of Johannes Buhrman), who arrived in America from Germany in 1767, were reinterred in the early 1900s in that graveyard. Those of his wife, Anna, and young daughter, too, were moved from the home farm, on Manahan Road near Camp David, to this final resting place. The presidential retreat is, in fact, on land once owned by Yost Wyant, father of Catherine Poorman, wife of John Poorman's son Henry. It was part of the "Three Mill Seats" tract.

Paul and Rita Gordon's *A Textbook History of Frederick County* tells of the influx of Germans, who came generally from Pennsylvania by way

The original Mount Bethel United Methodist Church, built in 1836, was known as the "Chestnut Bethel" church. *Courtesy of Leah Spade.*

of the Monocacy Trail, into Frederick County: "The Germans were described as industrious, honest, and God-fearing people. Having been driven from their country because of religious difficulties, the Germans took every opportunity to practice their faith. A place of worship was the focal point of the settlement, and thus Frederick County is blessed with a multitude of early churches whose records have been retained intact through the decades."

Needs other than spiritual were also met in the little community, however. The two-story building with the two-story porch, long a private home, was for many years the tavern in town or, more appropriately, a stop on the stage route. Many a traveler sought refreshment there after an exhausting trip to Baltimore by way of Emmitsburg or Thurmont. Around 1825 it was known as Hauver's Tavern. Wolf descendant and retired teacher Virginia Draper tells that later, before the Civil War, David Wolf operated the wagon stop. Still later, T.C. (Tom) Fox, who died in 1928, owned the place. At one time, the establishment was known as Black Horse Tavern.

General stores, too, have come and gone in Foxville, and Lobo's Market is the only one now conducting business there.

The *Frederick County Directory of 1886*, describes Foxville as follows: "situated near the Washington County line, 4 miles from Smithsburg… plenty of pure mountain water flows from never-failing springs; climate extremely healthy." A number of Foxville's inhabitants seem to attest to these benefits of location. Frederick resident and teacher Larry Hauver speaks admiringly of his distant relative—vigorous nonagenarian Alice Willard—who still maintains her mountaintop home there and enjoys quilting, while her brother, Clifford, at eighty-eight, continues to farm and cut timber.

Take a drive into the mountains, perhaps on Route 77, one day soon, and pass through the scenic terrain of Cunningham Falls State Park and Catoctin Mountain Park. When you get to Foxville's "square," it couldn't hurt to pause, breathe deeply of the rare air and then quench your thirst—with a sample of that legendary "pure mountain water!"

—*September 1991*

Utica's Covered Bridge: A Graceful Charmer

A lot of thirsty local people used to frequent the handsome yellow stone house in the dip on the left off Old Frederick Road, on the way to Utica. The building was unusually positioned directly over a large spring, and Mrs. Edna Buhrman, a village resident from 1925 to 1952, observes, "That was good for what they were going to do." She explains that while the place wasn't a saloon, the owner made liquor there. On the first floor operated a distillery, but the family resided on the second level and gained access by an outside flight of stairs. During the past couple years, new owners have been remodeling the sturdy structure, with the intention of converting the historic place into a guest inn.

The settlement known as Utica was long ago known as Utica Mills. Jacob Cronise, an enterprising gentleman, built a flourmill in the early 1800s and sold to customers in New York, Baltimore and Philadelphia. Located at the intersection of Old Frederick and Lewistown Roads, the mill was removed about 1918 and its broken-up stone used to increase the elevation of the road—subject to frequent flooding—which leads to the covered bridge. With the old Merchant Mill gone, Utica's one other industry also disappeared: most of the barrels made by Mr. Mohler and Mr. Devilbiss in the cooper shop across the road had been used to hold flour.

The record shows that Mr. Cronise engaged in considerable construction, for he built the first residence in Utica—the still-standing "mansion house"—and a store nearby, which also housed the tiny post office, moved to Lewistown in 1911. Both house and store are still in use, although the latter ceased operation as a business about 1944 and became a residence. Folks who need to make a quick purchase of an item or two can usually find what they want on the shelves of Connie and Odale Martin's friendly general store in neighboring Lewistown.

One of the most photographed places in Frederick County, and a colorful subject for many an artist, is the historic Utica covered bridge, a picturesque reminder of the horse and buggy days. Sturdily built from beams hauled to Fishing Creek from the wreckage of Monocacy-spanning Devilbiss Bridge, destroyed in the same storm system that caused the Johnstown Flood, the bridge at Utica became, at 101 feet, the longest such structure in Frederick County. A sharp-eyed individual walking through the covered bridge will be able to discern unused notches on some of the beams, revealing that they were part of material salvaged from the old Devilbiss Bridge; the workers had been unable to make a proper match.

In the early 1800s Utica schoolchildren learned the three R's in a log cabin on the site of what is now the cemetery. Until the building

Many beams in Utica's famous covered bridge were salvaged from the wreckage of Devilbiss Bridge. *Courtesy of the Historical Society of Frederick County.*

of the Lutheran and Reformed Union Church in 1838–39, the small schoolhouse, with a stone addition, served as both school and church. The community gained a two-room brick school in 1891, which consolidated with Lewistown in 1926. The first school bus, a wooden vehicle with hard bench seating, was owned and driven by R. Paul Buhrman. When he became sheriff's deputy, his wife, Edna, took over the route.

Eighty-eight-year-old Mrs. Buhrman recalls that water for the school had to be carried from a well in the little village, and it was "a glorious privilege, and a great way to get out of school," to be permitted to fetch the bucket of water. "Years later," she adds about an effort to be more sanitary, "the school was given a 'water cooler,' a thick lined container with a lid, with a spigot from which to draw water into our collapsible drinking cups. Of course, the water still had to be carried in a bucket from down in the village and poured into this cooler!"

In describing the schoolroom, Mrs. Buhrman says, "The teacher's desk was on an eight-inch platform at the front of the room. The desks were double, two children to a desk, an aisle dividing the girls from the boys. On Friday evening the floor was oiled to keep down the dust—no wall-to-wall carpeting in those days—and the little 'his' and 'her' buildings were at the extreme ends of the yard.

"We had no PTA, but the teacher would be invited as an honored guest to spend the night at various homes and happy were the children who could boast of having the teacher stay all night at their house."

Although a development of new homes has appeared, not a whole lot has changed, including the annual Utica picnic, held at Miller's Grove, east of Lewistown, a tradition for approximately 145 years. While the shiny bandwagon pulled by horses was long ago retired, there's plenty of other entertainment, and the country ham and fried chicken dinners, prepared and served under the direction of Mrs. Lucille Putman, with many volunteers, are as tasty as ever.

A visit to Utica this fall with camera in hand could reveal some pretty scenes and result in pictures to cherish of lovely old houses and a special red bridge that may not enhance the landscape forever.

—*October 1990*

Hardy Settlers Only Need Apply in Wolfsville's Wilderness

"When Dale and I were growing up, he lived across from the Morgan shop, and I grew up a mile up the road," remembers Mrs. Virginia Draper. "I went to Forrest School, and my grandfather ran the store at Garfield. But I never saw Dale until seventh grade commencement; the Sensenbaugh, Wolfsville and Forrest schools had come together for the occasion.

"In the fall of '31 Dale and I rode the school bus to Middletown High School together," Mrs. Draper continues. "Kids met the bus at Garfield. On Bidle's Hill, below Myersville, the bus picked up kids from Harmony. We all rode in one bus to high school. There have really been some changes since that time. But that's how isolated each community used to be."

A teacher until retirement ten years ago, she taught sixth grade for many years at Wolfsville Elementary School. Between 1970 and 1975, projects for her classes included going on history "safaris" and researching family histories. With the arrival, however, of more and more children from elsewhere, Mrs. Draper ended the genealogy program. Most of the old-timers in the area, she points out, are related.

On Garfield Road one finds a stone marker in memory of David Wolf Sr. and Nancy, his wife. According to the inscription, David, who died October 19, 1833, and his son Jacob Wolf Sr. were the co-founders of Wolfsville. Hoovers (Huber was the original spelling of the German name) also came early to this part of Frederick County, and there are people who believe the town could just as well have been called Hooversville or Hubersville. Indeed, President Hoover's ancestor was a relative, and the connection might have brought the village some attention. While the Hoovers were evidently religious leaders, the Wolfs were reportedly not averse to the making of strong drink.

Jim Snively is a Wolfsville newcomer. Residing in a house in the woods that was built perhaps twenty years ago, he is pleased with the location's privacy and quiet. Although he can see other houses from his property, he doesn't know his neighbors. But Jim is hardly isolated, for his car will take him to a major highway in a matter of minutes.

Such was not the case for those who settled here two hundred years ago. A trip by wagon to Frederick or Hagerstown took four hours. Yost Blickenstaff was the first owner of the Drapers' house, where they have lived since 1946. When the young man's brother in North Carolina got into financial trouble, Yost left his wife, Elizabeth (Ochs), and four or five children in the wilderness to go to the aid of his sibling and was absent for months. At that time, the nearest habitation was miles away. As Mrs. Draper tells the story, she registers no surprise that the young wife and mother hanged herself in 1780, after yet another baby arrived. The court determined that she had been mad for some time. The real mystery may be not why she took her own life, but how people managed to keep their sanity under such circumstances.

During World War II, Wolfsville began to lose its isolation. Some of the men got jobs away from the community; Fairchild was a major employer. Farms were at last getting electricity. Dirt roads were improved by crushed stone, produced on the spot by equipment methodically breaking up stone fences in the vicinity.

Customs that set the village apart—belsnickling or kriskingling by young people; serenading or "banding" every newly married couple; and tolling the bell for each year of life when a person died and again when the funeral procession approached the church—vanished some time ago, except from the memories of the oldest folks. "Every section has lost its quaintness and individuality," laments Mrs. Draper. "I blame TV," she adds.

Wolfsville boasted several makers of fine furniture: J.W. Morgan and his son Irving operated from the late 1800s to 1966, where the Ruritan

Columbus Stottlemeyer made this handsome curly maple chair at his Wolfsville shop in the early 1900s. *Photo by Ray S. Price.*

Park is now located; James Grove was a maker of coffins and furniture around the turn of the century; chairs by Fred and Columbus Stottlemyer were made from the late 1800s to the early 1900s and have been avidly sought after for their functional beauty and durability. The Morgan factory also produced a great deal of lumber for the building of Shangri-La (Camp David). Morgan of Morgan-Keller is a direct descendant, a great grandson, of factory founder James Morgan.

In 1969, the abandoned Stottlemyer factory was burned to the ground in a fire-fighting exercise. That same year, the village's last municipal music group, the Catoctin Community Band, played its final concert.

Ambitious attempts by Jacob D. Wolf to attract tourists to a fine hotel on South Mountain ended in failure. The Black Rock Hotel's inaccessibility on the Bagtown-Jugtown Trail drew few overnighters. Fires claimed the original building (1880) and the rebuilt structure (late '20s). The latter fire took with it two thousand wooded acres as well.

Wolfsville crossroads in 1942. Asa Stottlemeyer's place of business was to the left; Milton Harne's store had been in operation since the mid-1800s. *Private collection.*

Asa P. Stottlemyer's store ceased operation some years ago, but the old-fashioned country store bearing the name of Milton Harne still offers food and some merchandise to locals. President Roosevelt, while motoring to Shangri-La, would sometimes pause at this location on the crossroads of Wolfsville and Stottlemyer roads.

Wolfsville once had the reputation of being a town so rough that the annual Sunday School picnic required the presence of state troopers to deal with the men who had enjoyed too much moonshine.

Nowadays, a visit to Wolfsville at any season offers an impressive display of beautiful ruggedness not typical of the county. So far, the presence of those "from outside" has had only minor impact—and people with generations of kin whose final resting place may be on a nearby peaceful hillside hope the area can stay that way.

—December 1990

Rosebud Salve Puts Woodsboro on the Map

Woodsboro afforded one of the best stops for the stage coaches on the route from Baltimore to Creagerstown to the west or from the route north from Frederick to Lancaster and Philadelphia…It is a crossroads and as such has enjoyed a certain prominence." So wrote Frances Meehan Smith in *Woodsboro Remembers* (1976).

After the Civil War, the railroad came through; quarrying was conducted by the Barrick and LeGore families and "around 1890," according to Lawrence Dorsey in a 1976 newspaper article, "it was the Dodge City around here with those two hotels." Tales from that period indicate no shortage of poker games, liquor or dancing girls.

In the 1890s, the Glade Valley Milling Company opened. While the four-story mill just north of town stopped operating in 1957, the Circuit Rider shop occupied it for some years.

The well-known Powell brothers had ponds near Woodsboro, and in a good year they would send out a million goldfish.

Popular attractions in Woodsboro's colorful past included its outstanding baseball team and a concert band, among the best in the county.

But it was Smith's Rosebud Salve—produced by the Rosebud Perfume Company, organized in 1895—that really put the place on the map. As a young man, George F. Smith became a registered pharmacist and began formulating proprietary substances. His salve for minor skin irritations—and sore cows' udders—became so popular that the great volume of mail-

The Rosebud Perfume Company soon outgrew Dr. George F. Smith's original store. *The Robert S. Kinnaird Collection of Historic Thurmont Photographs.*

order business, with thousands of agents all over the country, necessitated the upgrading of the local post office from fourth- to first-class status.

On Main Street, across from the historic Woodsboro Savings Bank, founded in 1899, is located the original three-story Rosebud factory. It occupies what was formerly the Smith Hotel, and today it houses the company's mail-order division; the salve is manufactured elsewhere.

First named Woods Town, this village is about ten miles north of Frederick, near Israel's Creek and the Monocacy River. It was the northern part of a tract known as Monocacy Manor, a grant of 8,983 acres confiscated by the state in 1781 from Tory Daniel Dulaney. The 40-acre plat of Colonel Joseph Wood shows the settlement was designated in 1786 as Woodsberry Town. A later spelling became Woodsborough, and the present version is Woodsboro. The 1886 Frederick County directory also lists Woodsburg and Woodsboro.

Both town and district take their name from Revolutionary War officer Wood, whose sturdy home, constructed with Georgian lines, of brick imported from England, still stands on Cash Smith Road.

The 1886 population, of mostly Protestant German and English origin, was put at 350.

Anna Belle Smith Wickless, a Woodsboro resident all but eight years of her life, says more than five hundred people live there now. "It was a pretty busy town at one time. There was a lot going on," she recalls. Mrs. Wickless has pleasant memories of the roller skating rink, built in 1917. It became a popular spot for youngsters and was located in the building now used by Neoterik Health Technologies. "Oh, to me that was wonderful. We'd go up there on Saturday nights. Mr. Donsife owned it; he owned the blacksmith shop, too. At Halloween, we'd wear costumes. One time, I wanted something different. Mama sewed me a black dress with all these spoons on it. But when you fell down…"

During the first half of this century, the 225-seat Woodsboro Opera House served as town hall and social center. Mrs. Wickless remembers, "When I was a child, we saw movies there. Then I played piano for the movies for about four years.

"They used to have Chautauquas there, too. They'd come around, once a year, a whole week of Chautauquas, with one night something

Brothers Atho and Francis Donsife operated a blacksmith shop in the rugged tract then known as Woodsborough. *Courtesy of the Historical Society of Frederick County.*

historic on the program, another a comedy night—something different every day. They'd book the best that was available at the time."

Since 1953, the space, on the second floor of the bank, has been silent save for a few special events.

Lovely Victorian houses and a variety of businesses, within walking distance for most residents, give Main Street an appealing small-town flavor. Next time you're heading somewhere on Maryland Route 194, pause in Woodsboro and savor the friendly atmosphere.

—*December 1991*

Something in the Water: Yellow Springs Overflows with Bands

In the Tuscarora district, about five miles northwest of Frederick, stands the village of Yellow Springs. "The region is abundantly supplied with numerous springs of excellent water," states Scharf's *History of Western Maryland*. "Here also are the celebrated 'Yellow Springs,' 'Monotonqua,' or medicine-water, as it was called by the Indians." This writer relates that before the hunt or a battle, Indians of the Tuscarora tribe, long since vanished, "practiced, in conjunction with a free use of the water of the Montonqua, various charms and incantations to aid them in their enterprises."

The Indians had a strong belief as well in the healing and curative powers of these yellow springs, and each May, those with afflictions came to the medicinal water to bathe three times daily, to drink the oily blue substance shimmering on the surface and to apply to their bodies a plaster of the orange-colored sediment deposited by the flow from the springs.

Richard D. Costlow, present owner of the property on which the once revered spring is located, describes the pigmented material as "an iron colloid. This is what the Indians thought had a medicinal value. You don't see it until the water starts flowing. It looks like yellow cotton and settles to the bottom."

Originally, the farm where the yellow springs appear consisted of 165 acres and was evidently owned by George and Hannah Hedges Burkhart. Yellow Springs was a survey in 1754, but the place name does not appear until 1873 in the *Titus Atlas of Frederick County*.

T.C. Williams's *History of Frederick County* says the village is "located near the base of Catoctin Mountain. It was formerly known as 'Brooke Hill,' and derives its present name from the yellow springs in the immediate vicinity, a resort of considerable importance." A brittle and yellowed newspaper clipping from the first quarter of this century indicates that a part of the village of Yellow Springs was called Brook Hill, with a chapel and schoolhouse going by that same name. Schoolteacher George L. Twenty stated therein: "The name of Brook Hill is derived from the Reverend George C. Brooke, an eminent Methodist minister, who first preached in the open air to the residents of the place in the year 1850, and which led to the building of a log chapel for the purpose of holding religious services." The name continues to the present day in Brook Hill United Methodist Church on Indian Springs Road.

Early in the settlement's history, during the latter 1700s, the first paper manufactory in Maryland made its appearance on Tuscarora Creek. And a quarter of a mile from that site, also on the Tuscarora, three paper mills started operations prior to the Civil War. They produced wrapping, printing and writing paper, as well as bank-note paper.

The Frederick County Lima Bean Association, organized by James H. Gambrill Jr., who resided near Yellow Springs at the time, claimed another first for the community: the trial of cooperative buying in Frederick County.

Mention Yellow Springs, and many people think of bands bearing that name. In 1888, one of the county's best-known institutions began—the Yellow Springs Concert Band. For seventy years, Charles C.T. Stull Sr., who founded the music education program in the Frederick County schools, was a member of that popular organization; for sixty years, he directed it.

Another band long associated with the community was the Yellow Springs Little German Band, which performed over a wide area from the mid-'30s into the 1970s. "Old Professor" R. Donald Gearinger led the ensemble during most of its forty-year history.

Old-timers still recall community picnics, the H&F Trolley and the two-room schoolhouse, built in 1885, now the clubhouse of the Yellow Springs Lions and formerly the Yellow Springs Community Hall. A few folks may remember, too, when the village's main thoroughfare, called Hamburg Pike, was unpaved and often muddy and virtually impassable.

Yellow Springs was renowned for the bands bearing its name. *Courtesy of the Historical Society of Frederick County.*

Then, as now, the condition of a community's roads was of much importance. C.A. Staley, a prominent farmer, pointed out in 1922 that "the great need of our village is the repairing of the county roads. Land is becoming depreciated in value because of the bad conditions of the county road through Yellow Springs."

—December 1992

Eerie Le Gore Still Hides Secrets

It's always been a spooky place," says a Rocky Ridge resident about the bridge at LeGore. "Not at all like the covered bridges."

The five-arch stone bridge is certainly handsome, but there are no houses for some distance on either side of it, and dark woods along its approach contribute to feelings of unease. More than one person has committed suicide by jumping off the bridge, adding to the eerie atmosphere.

Eighty-three-year-old Marlin LeGore is well acquainted with the history of this 340-foot span over the Monocacy River. His grandfather, James William LeGore, built it. "The foreman on the bridge got two dollars a day—that was in about 1905," he says. "They had to put a road over the fields to get stone from the quarry out to the bridge, with mules. They wound a winch to lift all the stone. The foreman was an old 'Dutchman.' They used no blueprints, but drew with a stick in the sand and dirt. It took about four years to build it."

LeGore tells of trees being cut for scaffolding, before the actual construction could begin. "One tree fell and killed a man before they even got started." The builder's grandson also remembers tales about snakes: "They came out of everywhere when they worked on that bridge."

The bridge and surrounding area is, of course, named for the family that built it. In *Monocacy and Catoctin, Volume I*, a paragraph about the Huguenots includes the following: "When the Revolutionary War ended, some soldiers of the French troops who came with Lafayette

Construction of the 340-foot LeGore Bridge took about four years in the early part of the twentieth century. *Courtesy of the Carl Brown Collection, FCPL.*

and Rochambeau to aid the colonies in the struggle for freedom remained in America and became citizens of the new republic. The LeGore family represents this part of Frederick's population with French heritage and name."

Just north of Woodsboro, LeGore is a place long associated with stone quarrying. John LeGore went into the lime business at LeGore Station in 1861. In her book, *Woodsboro Remembers*, Frances Meehan Smith writes about the quarry operation:

> *In the early days limestone was quarried with hand tools. The stone was loaded on small carts pulled by trained mules who pulled the carts from the quarry up the hill to the burning kilns. They became so well trained that they could make the trip up and back on their own. The capacity of the plant was approximately 100,000 bushels a month and the annual sales amounted to over 700,000 bushels. Seventeen kilns were*

> *then operating, fired with wood, coal, and later coke. Shipments by rail, in boxcars, were made to North Carolina, South Carolina, Virginia, New Jersey, Delaware, Pennsylvania, and all over Maryland.*

From 1897 until 1976, a post office operated on LeGore quarry property, with company office and general store housed in the same 2.5-story building. The storekeeper took care of the mail. The pool table on the premises provided a focus for socializing.

Consolidation of LeGore Lime Company with two other firms formed the new Phoenix Inc. Smith's book notes that "the LeGore Quarry division of Phoenix no longer produced agricultural lime. Stone is instead sold for road building in Frederick County and other parts of Maryland."

S.W. Barrick & Sons Inc. is another important lime products enterprise in the area. In the early 1900s, this firm gained a number of skilled workers from Catoctin Furnace when that ironmaking operation shut down. Barrick built for its employees modest homes, a commissary and a church.

Children from this industrial community attended elementary school in Woodsboro. "The caretaker of the horses drove us in the carriage," recalls LeGore, "and he came and got us too. There was no water, no electricity. We carried water by bucket from the well." In referring to the use of privies, LeGore smiles as he says, "On Halloween we used to drag them around."

In the early 1980s, the bridge at LeGore underwent an overhaul requiring four months. Proportioned with both strength and grace, this structure has withstood numerous periods of high water—and even dynamiting many years ago. "No one knows who did that," says LeGore. Describing the act as politically motivated, he explains that there had been considerable dispute early on about where on the Monocacy to locate the limestone span.

This might just be the perfect spot to visit on Halloween night.

—*October 1992*

South

Growing Up or Growing Old, Buckeystown Is the Place to Be

As the large 1-270 sign came into view, a passenger in a car heading north gave a sudden happy shout and savored the town's name as he slowly read it aloud: "Buckeystown." Many years had elapsed since Sayyd Abdul Al-Khabyyr had visited Frederick County. But just for a moment he was no longer a sophisticated world-traveled musician about to close out a week of performances with Dizzy Gillespie at Blues Alley. He became, instead, seven-year-old Russell Thomas of a half-century ago, eyes moistening as he recalled wonderful times there with a beloved aunt. "They're all gone now," he said quietly, "but I'll never forget Buckeystown. My aunt even gave me the nickname 'Buckey' because I loved being there so much."

Although Sayyd and most of the other people acquainted with a younger Buckeystown reminisce fondly when memory is jogged and display great pride in the town's heritage, it has taken a relative newcomer with a passionate interest in the little place to record its colorful history for future generations. Nancy Willmann Bodmer's *Buckey's Town: A Village Remembered* has recently undergone its second revision and will again be available this fall. In her preface, she states that the book "was created initially from detailed information which was necessary for the town to be nominated to the National Register of Historic Places. Through the guidance of the Office of Historic Preservation, Frederick, and especially the assistance of Cherilyn Widell, the town was successful in achieving

Walter Specht needed a canoe to get around the town in August 1933. *Courtesy of Nancy Bodmer.*

this honored recognition." Widell was at that time a site analyst with the Frederick County Office of Historic Preservation.

Businesses continue to operate at the intersection of Buckeystown Pike (Route 85), which began as an Indian trail called the Conestoga Path, and Manor Woods Road, near where the Buckey brothers, who arrived in 1775, engaged in commerce; one was a blacksmith and the other a tanner. Both Indians and early settlers were attracted to this beautiful area by plenty of excellent water, particularly the Monocacy River and dependable springs, which still supply homes in the north end of town.

At times an abundance of water can turn into an overabundance, and townspeople vividly remember periods of flooding. Ed and Nancy Bodmer had just moved into their historic property at Buckeystown's crossroads, when Hurricane Agnes struck in June 1972. Nancy points to the kitchen table and says, "Water came over the top of it." She recalls that "the *News-Post* rook aerial photographs of different parts of the county, including here," during the flood. "Our post office had eight or ten feet of water in it." When all the old brass post office boxes had to be replaced, furniture store owner Walter Bernado salvaged a few and offered them for sale. A *Washington Post* magazine section advertisement stated: "Personal P.O.B. mahogany mail boxes for the defunct Buckeystown post

Nancy Bodmer, author of *Buckey's Town*, holds an old post office box salvaged from the flood of 1972. *Photo by Ray S. Price.*

office converted into banks, in limited quantity, combination lock, at Lord & Taylor, $100.00."

It is pointed out that the state marker about Carrollton, installed near the crossroads, is misplaced, for this tract was called Mount Hope and was not part of Carrollton Manor at all. Charles Carroll's Carrollton formed Buckeystown's west and south boundaries, and at the south end of town, a small portion of a Carrollton Manor lot was in the village at the close of the nineteenth century. The original four-hundred-acre tract, Good Luck, which made up the main part of Buckeystown, derived from a grant from the King of England in 1731.

On the corner near the erroneous sign stands a house renowned for its south wall. The *Frederick News* of September 30, 1939, relates that Frank Lloyd Wright stopped to admire its stonework while traveling

The original Buckeystown railroad station, built in 1831. *Courtesy of the Historical Society of Frederick County.*

through town. Annie and "Webb" Nicodemus owned this house which displayed, according to architect Wright, the "most beautiful wall in the United States."

Early this century the Nicodemus family's Velvet Kind ice cream and bricks from the Baker-owned plant were famous Buckeystown products. When Daniel Baker acquired the Buckey tannery and home in 1832, the legacy of this purchase was felt over the next century. Bodmer's book informs: "The Baker interests in the town besides the tannery involved a lime and stone business, a cannery, a school for boys just south of town, the Methodist Church, and numerous houses, buildings and farms."

Mrs. Rowena Hildebrand's parents have been here since 1922, and she has never lived anywhere else. "My daddy is almost ninety-eight now," she relates. "This was a very, very nice town, a good place to grow up in. There's a lot more traffic today, and everybody doesn't know everybody else the way they used to, but," she stresses, "it's still a very nice town."

—*November 1990*

Adamstown Welcomes Trains, Troops and the Occasional Diva

Except for raised voices over issues that endanger the community, such as recent battles against water contamination and quarry sites, life in this small, southern Frederick County village passes quietly, even uneventfully. But it wasn't always so. At times in its past, railroads, raiders and opera stars all stirred up some excitement in Adamstown.

The railroad gave birth to Adamstown in the early nineteenth century, even giving it the town's first name—Davis' Warehouse. Dr. Meredith Davis, owner of Greenfield Mills on the Monocacy and the area's first Baltimore and Ohio Railroad agent, constructed a storage building for his flour around 1836. The lone structure along the tracks soon became associated with the rail stop. In addition to the mill's product, trains carried good-quality locust wood cut from area farms to the coast, where it traveled to England for shipbuilding.

More buildings began to sprout up around the railroad until in 1840 settlers laid out a town. In his *History of Western Maryland*, J. Thomas Scharf notes that the town received its name in honor of Adam Kohlenberg, who was one of the first to settle there at the time. He claimed as his ancestor another Adam Kohlenberg who arrived in America with John Frederick Amelung, in 1784.

W.J. Grove's History of Carrollton Manor claims that the first settler in Adamstown was a black man, Robert Palmer. "He was a post and railer and in connection with setting up fence, ran a general store." But a letter to Grove from Reverend D. Guy Bready, who grew up in the village, described Palmer's occupation differently: "I can just remember the old log house which you state was the first building in Adamstown by Robert Palmer, colored. He was a shoemaker, and lived many years in his cabin about where the residence of Mrs. Arthur Cromwell now stands. Adam Kohlenberg built the first residence of logs and frame."

Twenty years later, national events electrified the community, causing a division among some townfolk. In the fall of 1860, as the clouds of civil war loomed, controversy over where the loyalty of a local unit of militia, the Manor Mounted Guards, should lie ended in the group's disbanding. Organized before the threat of rebellion, this crack cavalry company boasted as its members prominent Carrollton Manor farmers. But those pro-Union members protested this proposal: "Resolved, the Manor Mounted Guards and body offer their services, horses, and equipment to the Southern Confederacy and the troop as a whole for immediate departure."

When Federal troops entered the area and checked for hidden arms, "all houses of the members of the Manor Mounted Guards were searched and where found, their side arms and uniforms were taken," writes Grove in his book. The old company members, outraged by this act, met at Adamstown to discuss what they believed to be infringement on their rights. The Minute Men resulted—a new organization led by young Dr. Boteler, a physician in town. A recent graduate of the Virginia Military Institute, he soon left his fledgling practice to join the Confederate army.

When the war ended, life returned to normal in the hamlet. Businesses, such as canneries and banks, opened in town as the decades passed. "I was about twelve or thirteen when I went there to work," recalls ninety-three-year-old Ardella Young, employed as a housekeeper in Adamstown for many years and who still lives there. "They had stores, but the bank wasn't there then. One store was close to the railroad, and another was on the other side of the track. When I worked at the Thomases', after I did the dinner dishes I had nothing to do until time to get supper, so I'd go shuck a basket of corn at the factory. I'd get enough money to buy an ice cream cone or peanuts or candy from the store. Sodas were a nickel."

Then came another tragedy many folks can still remember—the failure of Adamstown's Central Trust Company, an early victim of the Great Depression. "I lost ten dollars when it went under," says Frederick resident Margaret Ringer, a member of the town's Biser family. "I was just a child, and it was all I had in the bank." Later, the Commercial State Bank moved into that building, which is now occupied by a restaurant.

A bright highlight in those dark times, and one that remained so in Adamstown's history, is the day in 1936 when the famous diva Lily Pons came to visit. The opera star put the town on the map with national news coverage of the celebrity event. Clarence Thomas, Ardella Young's employer, hosted a party for the distinguished guests, thrilling Mrs. Young. "I made a cake. I don't know how it tasted, but they ate it!"

With the departure of Ms. Pons and her entourage, a quiet settled back down over the community, leaving Adamstown in peace once again.

—*May 1993*

Mount Tabor Park in the town of Rocky Ridge is home to this lightning-fast wooden sliding board. It was rebuilt once, after a 1951 fire. *Photo by Davis Hall.*

Dating back to 1779, this building in Utica was known at different times as Eichelberger's Distillery and Price's Distillery. *Photo by Davis Hall.*

The congregation of Hopehill United Methodist Church has enjoyed the peaceful view from this location on Fingerboard Road since 1910. *Photo by Davis Hall.*

Each of the thirty-five squares in the "heritage quilt" displayed in the Providence United Methodist Church in Kemptown tells a story. *Photo by Davis Hall.*

Although the forge disappeared years ago, the blacksmith shop in Charlesville still stands at the crossroads near Tuscarora Creek. *Photo by Davis Hall.*

The three-story Rosebud Perfume Company is located in a former hotel in downtown Woodsboro. *Photo by Davis Hall.*

Adamstown resident Ardella Young earned spending money shucking corn at the cannery. This colorful label shows one of Frederick County's most popular agricultural products. *Courtesy of the Historical Society of Frederick County.*

Built in 1910 and expanded in 1917, the B&O roundhouse was the pride of the Brunswick rail yard. *Courtesy of the Historical Society of Frederick County.*

This C&O Canal Company promissory note for five dollars was issued in 1841. Bitter competition between the canal and railroad companies, dangerous work conditions and financing shortfalls all affected the way laborers were paid. *Courtesy of the Brunswick Railroad Museum.*

Architect Frank Lloyd Wright greatly admired the south wall of this Buckeystown home, pronouncing it the "most beautiful wall in the United States." *Photo by Davis Hall.*

Near Burkittsville stands the only monument in the world dedicated to war correspondents; it is inscribed with the names of journalists and artists who covered the Civil War. *Photo by Davis Hall.*

Above: Civil War correspondent George Alfred Townsend, who used the pen name "Gath," constructed all the stone structures shown in this postcard between 1884 and 1896. The unique War Correspondents Arch is now part of the National Park system, although it is surrounded by Gathland State Park. *Courtesy of the Carl Brown Collection, FCPL.*

Left: Main's was a popular place for socialization and locally made ice cream in Middletown. *Photo by Davis Hall.*

On a windy June day in 1914, a quickly spreading fire reduced much of Creagerstown to ruins. *Courtesy of the Historical Society of Frederick County.*

This rusted Frick engine, standing in front of the former Bittle's store in Ellerton, was once hauled wherever it was needed for sawmilling. *Photo by Davis Hall.*

Emmitsburg's Dinky Railroad was one of the smallest in the country, running just under eight miles in length. *Courtesy of the Carl Brown Collection, FCPL.*

A mill may have stood on this site by Catoctin Creek in Jefferson since the mid-1760s. In 1869, Basil Lewis bought the property. In 1977, the Lewis Mill's newest owners repurposed the structure as a pottery works. *Photo by Davis Hall.*

Lake View Hotel, once the pride of Lewistown, stood near what is now Route 15. *Courtesy of the Historical Society of Frederick County.*

Above: Visible from Middletown, South Mountain saw the first major battle of the Civil War in Maryland on September 14, 1862. Lieutenant Colonel Rutherford B. Hayes—elected president in 1876—is shown leading his regiment in the charge of the Twenty-third and Twelfth Ohio Volunteers against the Twenty-third and Twelfth North Carolina Volunteers. *Courtesy of the Historical Society of Frederick County.*

Left: The train station at Point of Rocks was once a quick stopover for trainloads of immigrants heading west. *Photo by Davis Hall.*

This imposing 1907 Sabillasville structure began as Maryland's first state-funded tuberculosis sanatorium. The property was repurposed in 1965 and now serves as the Victor Cullen Center for juvenile services. *Courtesy of the Historical Society of Frederick County.*

The Roddy Road Bridge was vandalized, then repaired, in the early 1990s. Located in Thurmont, it is one of Frederick County's three picturesque covered bridges. *Courtesy of the Carl Brown Collection, FCPL.*

In 1925, William and Grace Baumgardner turned a two-story farmhouse into the Peter Pan restaurant and introduced country-style dining to the Urbana area. The restaurant no longer exists, but locals still talk about fried chicken dinners enjoyed there decades ago. *The author's collection.*

The LeGore Lime Company quarry in 1955. As lime deposits were depleted, the company transitioned to production of crushed gravel. *Courtesy of the Historical Society of Frederick County.*

Contemporary visitors to Catoctin Furnace are invited to explore the ruins of the furnace as well as the nearby ironmaster's house. *Photo by Davis Hall.*

The Graceham Moravian Church is central to the community. *Courtesy of the Historical Society of Frederick County.*

Left: Dr. George F. Smith's Rosebud Salve is still produced by the Rosebud Perfume Company, organized in 1895. *Photo by Davis Hall.*

Below: In 1825, Thurmont brothers Jacob and Joseph Weller produced America's first friction matches. *The Robert S. Kinnaird Collection of Historic Thurmont Photographs.*

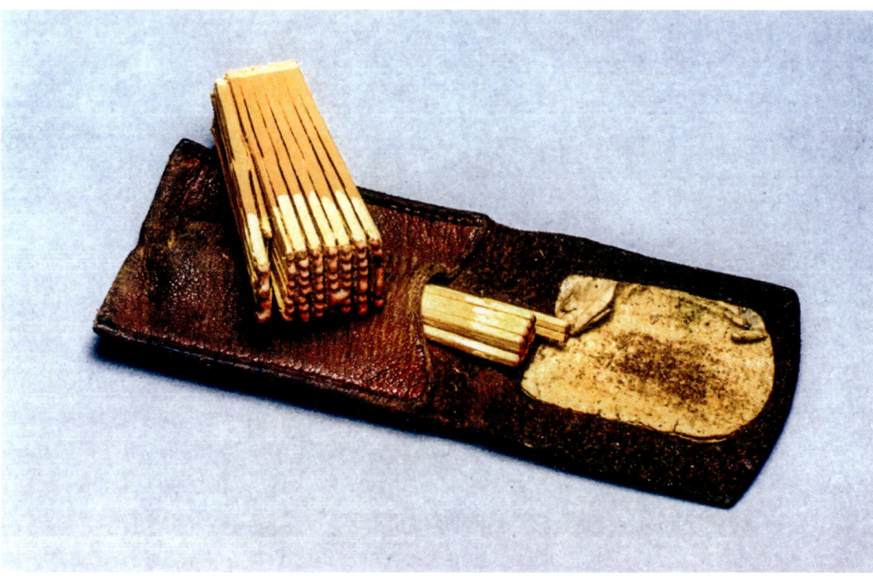

WHICH CENTERVILLE?

"Which Centerville?" the reader may ask. According to U.S. Postal Service information, the community here described bears an Ijamsville mailing address (21754). It is located in Urbana District on a stretch of Fingerboard Road (Route 80), up to Spencer's Lane, and on Ijamsville Road to just a bit past the church. Older folks tend to call the settlement Centersville.

The Centerville near Johnsville receives mail via Union Bridge (21791). Another Maryland county has a Centreville (21617), and Scharf's *History of Western Maryland* included a Centreville in a list of four villages in Middletown Valley: Jefferson, Centreville, Lander Post Office and Catoctin Switch. That (Middletown Valley) place name no longer exists.

Ebenezer United Methodist Church, a Registered Landmark, fronts Ijamsville Road near Route 80. Founded in 1883, and celebrating its 109th anniversary July 12, the building is the focal point of the hamlet and was constructed on property owned in the mid-1800s by John Howard. In her book, *History of the Nineteenth-Century Black Churches in Maryland and Washington, D.C.*, Nina Honemond Clarke says, "It was stipulated in the deed that this land was to be used for a church and operated in accordance with the Methodist Episcopal discipline by the heirs of Mr. Howard." The Addison family [heirs] did give land to the church trustees on which to erect a house of worship.

As a child, longtime Frederick resident Mrs. Mary (Foreman) DeLauter lived in Urbana near the town's main intersection. She remembers well having to walk all the way from her home to the one-room log Ebenezer schoolhouse in Centerville, the nearest "colored" elementary school. "We would walk to Sunday School, too," she says. "Sometimes it was terrible cold in the school." The potbellied coal stove in the middle of the room warmed only those sitting closest to it.

In the Frederick County Auditor's Report for 1916, we find listed Ebenezer School No.2, Colored. For instruction of her twenty-six pupils, Miss Ella Jones earned the sum of $260.79 that year. The fuel bill came to $29.57. Mrs. DeLauter recalls that the schoolteacher rented a room in a nearby home. The school was torn down years ago; the Men's Club of Centerville bought the property from the Board of Education and donated it to the church in 1969.

Mrs. Marcella V. Snowden Thompson, whose great-great-great uncle was John Howard, lived only a few houses away from the church. According to her daughter Mary Lyles, who still resides in Centerville, Mrs. Thompson used to say, "We live in Ebenezer." She was born in 1902 and died in 1991, but thanks to the 1979 oral history project of students at Governor Thomas Johnson High School, conducted under the direction of Anna May Hughes, Mrs. Thompson's stories live on in transcript and tape.

Like many of her neighbors, Mrs. Thompson walked to work in Ijamsville at Dr. Riggs's hospital, known today as Gabriel's French Provincial Inn. "You wouldn't believe it," she related, "but when I was thirteen years old I was cooking down there because they were short on help…and then when they were short of nurses I had to help carry the trays upstairs." She also recalled that she cleaned, "washed windows, wiped down the walls and all stuff like that. Then when canning time came we did all the canning. We put up corn, peaches, made jelly and things like that. They even did their own butchering."

The community probably dates back to the time of emancipation. In the cemetery adjacent to Ebenezer United Methodist Church, the oldest marked grave is that of Charlotte Fairfax, who died in 1872.

—July 1992

Industrial Lime Kiln Produces Concrete... and Beauty

History often repeats itself. A 1915 beauty contest afforded Lime Kiln unexpected and widespread publicity. Exactly seventy-five years ago May 17, the tiny town's name became a household word when lovely young Miss Clara May McAbee won "the prettiest girl in Maryland" title, traveled to California to enter the nationwide beauty competition and, in a close contest, placed second.

A letter written by William J. Grove to the *Baltimore News* on May 18 of that year reads as follows: "The beauty contest put the little village of Lime Kiln, Frederick County, on the map, nestled as it is on historic ground, Carrollton Manor, once owned by Charles Carroll, the signer of the Declaration of Independence. Why should not this beautiful girl win out, surrounded by the beauties of this old historic manor and softened by the southern breezes from the Potomac?"

Clara May's family lived but a stone's throw from the home of Grace Grove (Mrs. Sappington, now eighty-four, still of Lime Kiln), who relates that Mr. McAbee had a little store at the house—a liquor store. "It didn't look like much, but it served to sell booze in the old days," she chuckles. "On Saturday night I could sit on the porch at my mother's and hear the men going home happy." She smiles in recalling that "one stout gentleman in the town liked to go down to Mr. McAbee's and booze it up. If he didn't come home by a certain time, his wife would ask my mother and father to get the handyman to go after him. Since Will couldn't carry a man of that size, he'd just load him into his wheelbarrow and push him on home. And all the time Mr. Cutsail would be singing and having a good time!"

The McAbees' house still stands on Buckeystown Pike, but the part from which liquor was sold disappeared during remodeling a few years ago.

"The look of Lime Kiln hasn't changed very much, if you ignore the industry built up around it," says Bill Brosius, adding that "it was a compact little place." He grew up in Adamstown, but his Uncle Charles and some of his cousins were Lime Kiln residents. "The only thing there was the M.J. Grove Lime Company. They had their corporate headquarters there, and the road building department as well. My uncle was head of that division, and my father was assistant to him. They built bridges, too. They built the new bridge after the old Jug Bridge collapsed."

M.J. Grove also built the first concrete road in the state. It was south of Lime Kiln. Mrs. Virginia (Brosius) Thomas was one of his Lime Kiln cousins, and she reminisces fondly about living with her parents in the old Grove house, located right next to the railroad track. It, too, is still standing.

Mrs. Thomas recalls that travelers by horse and buggy would stop at the tollhouse on their way through town. "It sat right on the road, but when the widening was done to accommodate automobile traffic, in the early '20s, my father moved the house on up the road," she points out. Occupied and neatly maintained, it's easily identified today near the crossroads of Maryland Route 85 and Lime Kiln Road by its unusual roof.

In 1858, Manasses J. Grove built his first limekiln in town and also opened a general store. "The store was in operation there on the other side of the railroad tracks long before my time," comments Mrs. Thomas, born in 1912. "The lime company office was there, too, and the post office was attached to it. A lean-to against the store was the original Grove office. Then the office was expanded before 1930 into a two-story cement block building, which is now boarded up." She adds, "It used to be quite something."

A little farther up Lime Kiln Road, also on the right, one can readily spot the ruins of the kiln. Mrs. Thomas describes how the elevated ramp allowed mules to unload their wagons full of stone directly into the kiln, where a high quality burnt lime resulted from the wood firing. And

Lime Kiln's tollhouse can still be seen on Md. 85. *Private collection.*

nearby was the quarry. When the desirable stone ran out, quarries in Frederick and Steven City, Virginia, became the sources of supply.

Both Mrs. Sappington and Mrs. Thomas delighted in describing the village's one-room school. It was located next to the long-since abandoned Methodist church. The boys' cloakroom was on the left, the girls' on the right. There was no plumbing, remembers Mrs. Sappington, and no well. "The well was almost up to the railroad track. Kids would be sent to the well with a bucket. It was fun to get the water, because you didn't have to go to school then! The children would bring their own collapsible aluminum cups to use."

Mrs. Thomas found it amusing that red-haired Mr. Calvin Hoffman used to ride his bicycle up the track from Adamstown, to teach the youngsters at Lime Kiln.

Long ago referred to as "Slabtown," from the slabwood houses put up for railroad construction crews, Lime Kiln reveals to visitors glimpses of a rich past, rapidly vanishing. Take a camera along, and include the village during a leisurely Sunday excursion. It's well worth the time.

—*May 1990*

Sleepy Little Doubs Wasn't Always So

Tucked away in a rural, wooded area ten miles south of Frederick and one mile west of Adamstown, the tidy village of Doubs once hummed with the noise of a flourmill, the clanging of engines and the whine of train whistles. But Doub's Station, established in 1885, and the mill, built in 1812, are gone, and trains do not pause there anymore.

Today, traffic is so light in Doubs that in the evening it is not unusual to see a cat or two lying comfortably in the middle of the road. Residents cavalierly park their cars well into the roadway, confident no state trooper will ticket there, nor will they impede any other traffic. It was not always this mellow in Doubs.

Some communities might not want to own up to having been named after a fellow like Jacob Doub, once described as "an old bachelor and a very rough, hard-swearing Dutchman." He acquired the flourmill and set to work waking up Doubs. He persuaded the B&O Railroad to put in a switch, or spur, across from the mill to facilitate his shipments of flour. Mill workers and residents started calling their town Doub's Switch.

Doubs originally was part of Carrollton Manor, the seventeen-thousand-acre land grant deeded to Charles Carroll in the early settlement of Maryland. Carrollton Manor included the hamlets of Adamstown, Buckeystown, Licksville, Lime Kiln, Tuscarora and Doubs.

Charles Carroll owned many slaves, although, according to Robert J. Brugger, historian and author of *Maryland, A Middle Temperament*, Carroll

Children from Doubs walked to the Doubs Elementary School in Pleasant View. In this 1919 class portrait, Arnold DeLauter stands in the second row, to the right of his teacher, Lillian Proctor. Margaret Lawson (Whelan) stands in the front row, second child from the right. *Courtesy of Arnold DeLauter.*

was one of several prominent Marylanders who spoke out against slavery and "stood on the side of education and accomplishment" for blacks.

Perhaps because of the large number of slaves held in the area, Doubs had a considerable concentration of black residents in the early 1900s. Margaret Lawson Whalen, eighty-three, has lived in Doubs most of her life. She remembers getting up early as a child and walking to Carey town to attend the "colored" school at Pleasant View called Doubs School.

"I think so much about it in the wintertime," she says, "The roads were frozen. We wore boots and had to carry our shoes."

Margaret and her husband, Roger, moved to town when they married at the ages of twenty and eighteen. Now eighty-five, Roger worked for forty-seven years with the B&O Railroad. The couple remembers when Doubs was a bustling place with three stores, a post office and a tavern. "There used to be a beer joint here, right by the railroad track," says Roger, pointing to a spot near the intersection of Doubs and Pleasant View Roads. "I took the owner [of the tavern] to Frederick every Saturday morning. He wouldn't shop any other place than Carmack's. He and I were just like that," Roger illustrates with intertwined fingers. "But he wouldn't let me in his place to get a bottle of beer. He wouldn't let any black people in there."

The mill at Doubs offered employment for many residents. It closed in 1968, but eighty-seven-year-old Arnold Delauter remembers hauling wheat to the mill as a fourteen-year-old. "The good Lord had to be with me," he says. "I worked for this farmer who had six horses and a wagon with sideboards on it. I'd load the wheat, and with six horses I had to go down this hill. There was a bridge at the foot of the hill. I'd have to talk to the horses to get around there, so the wagon wouldn't go into the creek."

In 1879, Lewis Specht opened the village's first store, which sold both liquor and groceries. Many people ran the small store over the years, like Joshua C. Michael, who also was the freight and express agent for the railroad as well as postmaster for the town. Other stores opened and closed throughout the years. All the stores remain today as residences, but the tavern was torn down.

The Whalens say they miss the stores and post office, which closed January 1, 1969. But the now-quiet Doubs lives on in their memories as the active town it once was.

—April 1994

Life in Hopehill: Hard Work and Generous Hearts

Bernard Brown grew up in Hopehill. His roots remain deep in this tiny rural community located halfway between Buckeystown and Urbana, although he has resided in Frederick for many years and been a member of the Asbury United Methodist Church since his marriage. Yet Hopehill United Methodist Church is still "his church" and his sisters retain ownership of their grandfather's place in the village. "We wanted to keep it in the family," he explains. Now retired, Brown, sixty-three, contemplates moving himself and his wife, Ruth, into the property someday, so he can really return home.

Situated astride the intersection of Fingerboard and Hopeland Roads, this little place called Hopehill is not likely to show up on local maps. Like so many other communities originally settled by blacks, Hopehill does not have its name and history recorded in the usual places associated with the keeping of archives. Instead, it exists in the memories of old-timers and, often, in the booklets compiled by local churches, the heart and soul of settlements like Hopehill.

One of nine children, Brown reminisces about his childhood in Hopehill. "Regardless of how young you were, you didn't sit around. On our place, as far back as we could remember, along with the Lee family, we raised our own chickens. Daddy would have as many as one hundred shoats and pigs. He started raising beef cattle, too." His father also grew corn for the Buckeystown factory and a field of peas for the

Jenkins brothers' cannery in Frederick. "I can't remember being without something to eat because we raised it all ourselves," he remarks.

Mrs. Jennie Weedon Lee, a ninety-one-year-old resident of the community, says that she and her husband were seasonal employees of the Buckeystown plant, closed since the Second World War. "I ran a shucker there," she recalls. "Then I was doing cans." Mr. Brown mentions that his mother and many other women of Hopehill worked there during the season.

Bessie Lee Brown, retired from her federal government job in Washington, D.C., and living with her mother, Mrs. Jennie Lee, speaks of the "beautiful store" owned by Edgar Diggs. "Most of the people of Hopehill shopped at that store. There was no other place to go." She notes that it closed in the 1950s and then "just fell down."

Church was another institution important to the community. Located on Park Mills Road, the first house of worship for nearby residents was Hopehill Methodist Episcopal Church, a log structure covered with weatherboard painted gray. Dating back to before 1868, "the log church had been handed down from the white folks to the black folks of Hopehill," according to Hopehill United Methodist Church's history booklet written for its seventy-second anniversary celebration in 1982.

When attendance at the old church declined and the structure sold for what the lumber was worth, parishioners began to meet in the log schoolhouse, which stood across from the present church. In 1910, land purchased from the Baker family provided a site upon which to erect that attractive house of God still in use, Hopehill United Methodist Church.

In the original schoolhouse, black children from neighboring Buckeystown and Flint Hill joined the Hopehill youngsters for lessons. Mrs. Lee remembers the old log school's use for all social gatherings. Her family owns the second schoolhouse built in Hopehill; it closed in 1959 when integration occurred and pupils then traveled to Urbana for their elementary education. The county auditor's report of 1916 listed the mother of Mrs. Jennie Lee, Florence "Jennie" Weedon, as a teacher at "Hopeland School (Colored)," along with James Whitten.

Until twenty years ago, Hopehill, Ebenezer, Bell's Chapel and Fountain Mills' churches were all part of the Centerville charge. Mrs. Lee points out that "walking to and from services in Centerville sort of kept an everlasting friendship between the communities." But in 1973, with smaller churches closing and some merging, Hopehill joined the Buckeystown charge, which includes Pleasant View, Sunnyside and Buckeystown.

Hopehill's congregation continues to remain a visible and strong presence in a changing population. It seems to exemplify the words of Nina Honemond Clarke, who wrote *the History of the Nineteenth Century Black Churches in Maryland and Washington, D.C.*, when she observed, "Remember, the church is the alpha and omega of the black community."

—*February 1993*

Improving "Maryland's Worst Road" Changes Urbana Forever

"I don't know where in the world I'd rather be than right here," says Mrs. Eurath Ann Selckmann, past president of the Urbana Civic Association. "And we all know one another, between school and churches, even though we're spread out in the community."

Folks living in the Urbana area claim there are no set boundaries for the unincorporated village and favor the term Urbana District, which includes such places as Park Mills, Flint Hill, Hopeland, Centerville and Thurston. In the nation's bicentennial year, 1976, the Urbana Civic Association compiled a booklet recording some of the early history of the Urbana election district, settled around 1725 largely by people of English background. Older residents maintain that Wooltown was the original designation for Urbana, but nobody seems to know for sure the circumstances under which that name was supplanted.

Not long ago, a *News-Post* article described Urbana as follows: "At present, the village is but a cluster of old houses, an elementary school, a firehall and a couple of businesses around the intersection of Md. 80 and Md. 355, a few yards from the 1-270 exchange. Fewer than 100 people live in the village now." Early written accounts of Swiss explorers in the countryside extolled the view from nearby "Pain de Sucre"—Sugarloaf Mountain. Others who had business in the plainlike surroundings appreciated as well the view of this 1,282-foot residual hill of the Appalachian chain, and some stayed to build houses facing the forested feature. In the 1700s, Thomas Johnson, Maryland's first elected governor, owned Sugarloaf; his youngest brother, Roger, later acquired it. In its shadow on the western edge, the first of many commercial users, Roger Johnson's iron furnace, made an impact on the mountain—a ready source of fuel.

In 1925, William and Grace Baumgardner turned a two-story farmhouse into the Peter Pan restaurant and introduced country-style dining to the area.

The charcoal from stately trees cut on its slopes and the exceptional silica Sugarloaf yielded also fed an industry opened on Bennett's Creek in 1789: John Frederick Amelung's New Bremen Glassmanufactory. Amelung's glassworks was one of the leading manufacturers in America.

In 1780, Roger Johnson built a mansion called Wellcome Farms facing Sugarloaf Mountain on the tract Resurvey of Right and Good Reason. According to present owner Ethel Loeb, parlor cabinets and many windows still display original Amelung glass.

Roger Johnson purchased in 1808 a property not far from that home. It was named Plummer's Delight; son Richard resided there. It seems appropriate that the present owners are both doctors, as Dr. Benjamin Hughes maintained an office in the fieldstone house with roof of local slate, which he bought before the Civil War. Drs. Martha and Gerald Schipper relate, "Dr. Hughes was a large slave-owner. His slaves operated this farm. Many of his horses were stolen during the war. Then he freed his slaves before the war's end, losing most of his wealth."

The Schippers' son Martin points out that "there was a lot of slave trading in this area, as people could buy slaves cheaper here." Martin, whose field of historical expertise includes the Urbana District's early agriculture, tells that "a lot of tobacco, a labor-intensive crop, was grown here when prices were good. Tobacco prices went down after the Civil War."

Originally, the road offering access to the home of Richard Johnson passed by the other side of the property. But through citizens' contributions of land and money in 1887, Dixon Road came into being. Not heavily trafficked over the years, it stood in low priority for paving. In 1959, however, at the insistence of the Schippers, who were willing to pay the cost of the materials—$5,000—for blacktopping, Dixon Road was improved. "It cost the county much more than $5,000," says Gerald, who feels the family got a bargain.

The Farm Neighbors League, back in 1937, did not find their demands so readily met. According to the *Daily News* on August 11 of that year, the group mounted a "program of merciless publicity…to shame the State into repairing what the 'Neighbors' call Maryland's worst road… The farm neighbors had a large sign erected at the top of the hill just beyond Araby on the Urbana pike calling attention to the fact that this 'most famous bad road' lies just five miles beyond, within forty minutes of the nation's capital."

Many homes in Urbana and Urbana District are of considerable historic and architectural significance. Many-in-One, for example, once housed the hamlet's post office, closed in 1910. Fat Oxen is one of the oldest homes in Frederick County, dating back to before the Revolutionary War. Landon was built in Virginia in 1754, then transported piece by piece from that site and put together in Urbana ninety-two years later. For years a young ladies academy, later a military school for boys, until the Civil War the structure served General J.E.B. Stuart briefly as a headquarters, and both sides in the war used it as a hospital.

During a certain era in our country's history, many residences concealed equipment for producing alcoholic beverages. Martha Schipper recalls, "When we moved in, we found a still in the basement, and there were barrels full of corn mash here!" Martin refers to tales of "another still across the hill, and shotgun fights over the fences. The people across the way got arrested."

While Zion Episcopal Church, built in 1802, may be one of the first two buildings in Urbana, a much younger place continues to put the village on the map. Mr. Jesse Dixon's description of its 1854–55 construction on land "embowered in trees and shrubbery" appears in *History and Legend, Urbana District, 1976*. According to this booklet, "the eight-room brick house was 'L' shaped and was quite a showplace." Up until rather recently, the Baumgardner family owned this landmark house, greatly enlarged and made famous as the Peter Pan Inn.

Landscape-altering growth is going to affect Urbana District. Indeed, one resident pointed out that "visitors to the area will pass along roads just waiting for developers to get in." Take the time on a crisp autumn day to explore some of the area's byways. They will offer glimpses of a past that may soon become precious in memory.

—October 1991

Awakening to a Rooster's Crow in Pleasant View

That most basic of country voices—the crowing of a rooster—is not a part of the environment for most children today. In scattered, less congested Frederick County communities, however, one can still pause and hear sounds associated with the land, rather than the city's endless traffic and the cacophony of different musical tastes. Such a place is Pleasant View, a little settlement usually overlooked by people in their haste to fulfill errands in nearby Doubs or Point of Rocks.

Arnold DeLauter, a respected resident of Frederick for over sixty years, grew up there and would be astir even before the roosters began their "song." "You'd get up in the morning, you'd have so much to do before going to school," he remembers. "I'd milk the cows and feed the chickens and hogs." Born in 1906, the oldest of six children, he found little time for play. But the winters of his childhood sometimes provided a form of recreation universally enjoyed by the young: "We'd sled until one or two o'clock in the morning," he says. "The moon would be shining so light, and you could see for miles."

The first school was a one-room structure, with one teacher conducting lessons for seven grades. There, Mr. DeLauter received his formal education. "They didn't have any high school for colored kids," he says quietly.

Called Doubs Schoolhouse, although located in Pleasant View, the brick building that replaced the original school, on the same site, was years ago converted into a church.

Prior to desegregation in 1956, African American children traveled from nearby towns to attend the Doubs Elementary School in Pleasant View. This brick building replaced the original 1902 one-room structure in the 1950s. *Courtesy of the Historical Society of Frederick County.*

For the community's black students, only one hundred days of attendance a year were required—several dozen fewer than what was demanded of white schoolchildren at that time. "You could come out the fifteenth of April to go to work," recalls DeLauter. "The farmer wanted you there then; he wanted me to help his wife put the garden out." In the fall, "you had to be in school by November. It was dark by this time of year. You'd need a lantern to see to finish the chores." DeLauter was then around ten years old.

According to Nina Honemond Clarke's *History of the Nineteenth Century Black Churches in Maryland and Washington, D.C.*, the town was founded by Patrick and Henrietta Ambush. They purchased their land from Ben White, a white farmer, who owned the Mooreland stock farm; it encompassed what became Pleasant View.

Area roads were either mud or dust. With the advent of the automobile, "if a car went through, you'd see the women running out, taking their clothes down off the line!" tells DeLauter.

A post office never opened there. Earliest delivery of mail was by buggy. At times when the snow was so deep that it closed up the road, the mailman would get on the horse and ride his route through town.

Born in Doubs but a longtime resident of Pleasant View, Royal Lawson successfully pushed to have the street through the settlement paved. He ran the only store the community has ever had. It was situated on a rise by the side of Pleasant View Road. "Little country stores couldn't make it after the big chains came in," he comments. "People have to go to Adamstown or Point of Rocks to shop now." He tore down the building several years ago.

In 1956, desegregation of the public school system was starting to take place in Frederick County. Integration was achieved throughout most of the county by 1962. David Young, who lives in Doubs, points out that the little school in Pleasant View, however, was the last all-black elementary facility in Frederick County. It remained in use until March 1964, when Carroll Manor School opened its doors; Young was at that time in the fourth grade.

Royal Lawson (Sr.), a school bus driver for years, is proud to have driven the first desegregated vehicle in the county—a job that was not easy in the beginning. He took the children into Frederick.

On a curve in the road is located the focal point of the tiny settlement: Pleasant View United Methodist Church, built in 1910 by the people of the community. Reverend J. Sherman Mason currently ministers to the congregation. Clarke's book states:

> *In 1890, they began to make plans to build a church. Patrick Ambush and Richard Harris gave the land. Claude Delauder began to haul stones in his horse-drawn wagon from Ben White's farm. They began to build a stone foundation for their church. Before this job was completed the members had a disagreement and the work stopped.*
>
> *Twenty years passed and the partial foundation stood there. Under the leadership of the Reverend Roedock the work on the church began again.*
>
> *Beginning in October 1910, Claude Delauder went through the same routine of hauling more stones from Ben White's farm to complete the foundation of the church. This time the church was completed and the families of Pleasant View rejoiced. They were proud of their ability to work together in harmony to build this lovely little church.*

That vista mentioned by DeLauter still exists. While so many areas in Frederick County have lost their pastoral scenes, Pleasant View (so

Members of the United Methodist Church's small but active congregation in 1991 included *(left to right)* Ardella Young, Arnold DeLauter, Mary DeLauter, Anna Brown, Dorothy Lewis, Velma Lawson and Vernon Proctor. *Photo by Ray S. Price.*

named by a man of the gospel, the Reverend Bean), has retained its, well, pleasant view of the countryside. It is best appreciated if the passerby will take a moment to stop, look and even listen on Pleasant View Road's high point. In any season, the visitor is assured a pleasant experience.

—*February 1991*

Point of Rocks Sits Next to—and Occasionally Under—the Mighty Potomac

"When you work in the post office for thirty-nine years, you know everybody, you hear the good things and bad, and you have to be a good listener," says Mrs. Cornelia Hickman, who used to serve as Point of Rocks' postmistress. Now eighty-nine and enjoying a project-filled retirement, she describes how the first post office she managed fared during floods: "The water got not quite up to the ceiling, and it was a high ceiling. I'd bring everything here to my house. It was an awful job to wash the mud out. 1936 and 1942 were the worst; '72 wasn't too bad. The post office was on the other corner then. A man came in a motorboat and took me to the building."

According to a January 19, 1934 *Blade-Times* (Brunswick) article written by her:

> *At the foot of Catoctin Mountain where the range meets the beautiful Potomac River and the Chesapeake and Ohio Canal is located Point of Rocks—a town of beauty with a population of 500. The town received its name from the peak that for years projected over the C&O Canal. Due to this projecting boulder, canal boats could not pass at this point. It was removed by the C&O Canal Company years ago. It is said that this huge boulder was rolled down the mountain by Confederate troops during the Civil War in order to obstruct the Baltimore and Ohio railroad traffic at this point.*

Cleanup after the memorable flood of 1889. *Courtesy of the Historical Society of Frederick County.*

Retreating Confederate troops also burned the first bridge at Point of Rocks. Four spans of the 1889 bridge, as it was nearing completion, were carried downstream during the same severe weather system that caused the Johnstown Flood. The present structure was built following another destructive flood in 1936.

A yellowed newspaper clipping of August 19, 1922, explains that the village was at one time named "Trammelstown" and situated about a mile from its present location. A blaze affecting much of the community brought about its removal, aided by the B&O Railroad, to a new site, where it was renamed Point of Rocks.

At one time an active center of trade, Point of Rocks gathered freight destined for shipment to Baltimore.

Before the turn of the century, hundreds of boats operated on the C&O Canal, which served as an important transportation system. Long dry, with mature trees standing in its overgrown bed, the canal is now maintained by the National Park Service, with the tow path enjoyed by hikers.

"My uncle and father had a little restaurant by the railroad depot," recalls Mrs. Hickman. "They used to sell ham sandwiches. Grandmother would cook the hams, and she made the most delicious apple and peach pies." Coffee, carried in a copper bucket onto the trains as they paused in the station, was dipped from the large container into small tin cups, which were brought along with sugar, milk and rolls in a basket. "People got to keep the cup," Mrs. Hickman explains, "because in those days there was no plastic or styrofoam." Continuing, she describes how "my uncle and daddy would have to jump off sometimes when the train started up, and that was very dangerous."

Mrs. Hickman adds, "Trainloads of immigrants from Ellis Island came through here, heading for the West. They'd always stop and get sandwiches and coffee."

The family purchased tin cups by the box from Lewis A. Rice Company and tobacco products from Albert Condon, both in Frederick. Mrs. Hickman mentions that local educator Mary Condon Hodgson was his daughter.

Cornelia Hickman displays the copper bucket used many years ago in serving coffee to train passengers who paused at Point of Rocks. *Photo by Ray S. Price.*

Frederick resident Mary Herber remembers what it was like to live in Point of Rocks between 1971 and 1981: "We had a really big flood in 1976. Water went up to five feet in the house, but the foundation height brought that up three or four more feet. People were laughing at me the day before, when the kids and I moved everything upstairs, but I had a feeling we were going to be flooded."

At that time, she had a poodle, a collie with eight puppies and five children. "When we had to leave, the dogs all went to my mother's, with three of the children, for a month, but I had the oldest boys with me. My mother nearly went crazy."

Describing how neighbors helped those who were flooded out, she says, "People came with food—for a month. We had no electricity all that time, Porta-Potties were set up and water was trucked in by the National Guard. No officialdom," she stressed. "The people did it themselves. It took all that summer to put the house back in shape."

While the Herber children were bused to school in Adamstown and then in Frederick, Point of Rocks children of an earlier time attended school in their own village. The older, three-room schoolhouse has been converted into two apartments, and the present Community Center was the last school built in town.

Mrs. Hickman rode not a bus but the B&O train to attend Girls High School in Frederick and then Hood College.

Although the two hotels once filled with hundreds of anglers are long gone—and the record shows that President Cleveland enjoyed bass fishing here—folks still come to Point of Rocks to fish, and snacks are available in small local stores.

Of this little community by the river, Mary Herber says, "It was a good place for kids to grow up. They played by the canal, on the big hill over the railroad tunnel and in wide-open fields. There were caves to explore; they fished. Everybody knew all the kids, and they didn't get away with a lot. It was a protected environment, old-time, make-believe America."

After a visit to Point of Rocks, you may be of the same opinion as the Reverend Dr. T.S. Baker, first rector of St. Paul's Church. Over one hundred years ago, he said that although he had seen the famous highlands of Scotland and experienced a trip down the Rhine River, no landscape he viewed surpassed that of Point of Rocks.

—August 1990

East

There Will Always Be a Kemptown

Blackberries are sold on the honor system here, from unattended roadside tables. A sign invites customers to leave a dollar in a tin can in exchange for a pint of the tart fruit. According to Cliff Falcon, who has lived in Kemptown since 1975, the system is not abused. "People are very friendly here," he notes. "We've lost some of the elderly recently, though," he observes. "Part of the town's history went with them."

Living in an approximately one-hundred-year-old frame home on the corner of Kemptown Church Road and Fingerboard Road (Maryland Route 80), Falcon also owns the picturesque property next door and describes the log cabin as having been at one time the Molesworth Funeral Home. "A lot of people stop to photograph it," he says.

Across the road stands another log structure, long covered by siding, but readily pointed out by local people as the place where President Lincoln once stayed overnight during the Civil War. Marianne Browning, eighty years old, is especially interested in that story, as it was her great-grandparents, Mr. and Mrs. John T. Lewis, who graciously hosted Abraham Lincoln as he ate and rested in their home, the second residence built in Kemptown.

It was on August 1, 1801, that Solomon Kemp purchased 123 acres from John Pidgeon in what was known as "Snakeroot Thicket and Nattlewood Forrest" and began to farm. Parcel by parcel, Kemp sold off his land, and the developing agricultural community came to be known as Kemptown. Although Kemp's house is gone, another stands on the attractive site.

As the hamlet grew, a central and dependable source of well water was needed. In *Memories of Kemptown*, published by the Providence United Methodist Church, Mrs. F.D. (Nicie) Browning described the project:

> *Digging wells in those days was very slow; pick, shovel and rock powder were used. Dirt was taken out by windlass and tub. They worked, at times, on the well for about two years, getting down about 55 feet—and no water yet! Becoming discouraged, it was decided to have a man with a spring pole drill to finish the job. He drilled a hole four inches in diameter and 22 feet deep in the old dry well. This gave them plenty of water, and it became known as the "town pump." So happy were the people that several wanted to go down to the bottom to see the water. Rebecca Lewis Hillery, then a young girl, went down in the tub that had been used to draw out the dirt.*

Marianne Browning points out that the well is on the dividing line between the house in which Lincoln stayed and the property next door. "It was in use for the town until the hard road was put through. Something was put on top to close it up, but it could be used again," she comments.

While commercial ventures serving the community have come and gone, and townsfolk may speculate as to the precise location of some businesses, such as the blacksmith shop, there are for the most part memories long enough and evidence in abundance to indicate exactly where they were in operation. Plummer Davis's general store originally occupied what has been for the past ten years Chuck and Evelyn Doylan's Kemptown Store. And older people can remember when Raymond Loun started his junk dealership fifty years ago. After his death, his widow and sons took over the business.

Maxine Browning, seventy-six years old, tells of a somewhat unusual amusement the local children enjoyed when Kemptown had a mortuary in the old log cabin: "The undertaker's living quarters were in a building behind it, and in between the two was what we'd call a breezeway now, where the hearses were kept, a black one for the adults and a white one for the children. The undertaker made coffins; my grandfather also made them there. When we were children, we would play in the coffins, hiding inside when they were standing on end!"

"After the undertaking business moved, my grandfather used the place as a carpenter shop for a while," she recalls.

Miss Browning's sister, Mary Elizabeth Browning, taught Kemptown youngsters for many years in school No. 6. In 1932, however, the one-room building was closed, and the area's children have since that time attended school in New Market.

Much of the community's activity has been centered at the Providence United Methodist Church, now pastored by warm and enthusiastic Laura B. Easto. Her husband, David, describes a heritage quilt project as "real important to the women of the church. Each square represents something of significance in Kemptown, such as the first meetinghouse, the first telephone, the first stained-glass window. They started it last year, and it will be hung in the church hall in October."

Since 1955, church members have continued the American festival tradition of apple butter boiling. Laura Riggs Burke wrote in *Memories of Kemptown*, "Several days and evenings are spent in preparation of

Among the many contributors to the "heritage quilt" were lifelong Kemptown residents Marianne Browning and Maxine Browning. *Photo by Ray S. Price.*

the apples, but the delicious meal prepared on boiling day for about 60 people and the satisfaction of supplying repeat customers, as well as church families, with another year's supply of apple butter makes it all worthwhile."

While you may have missed the annual and highly successful Sunday School dinner picnic last month, with music in the evening by the Browningsville Band, another opportunity to enjoy some wonderful country cooking—an all-you-can-eat turkey and oyster dinner—will take place in late winter on the first Saturday in March.

Although development is moving in, the townspeople, in their *Memories of Kemptown*, express confidence that "friendliness and neighborliness, caring and sharing, consideration and kindness, will hold together the community we love so much, and there will always be a 'KEMPTOWN.'"

—*September 1990*

Industrious Ijamsville Knocks One Out of the Park

During the first half of the nineteenth century, probably the most exciting day for the village folks was Thursday, March 13, 1832, when four B&O cars, each drawn by a single horse and with eighty passengers aboard, on the first historic journey from Baltimore to Frederick of America's oldest railroad, passed through "Ijam's Mill." So wrote Charles E. Moylan, associate judge, Supreme Court of Baltimore City, and Ijamsville native, in his 1951 *Story of a Country Village*. A far cry from interstate travel today, the journey from Baltimore to Frederick required eight hours and cost $1.80.

In the first half of the twentieth century, the community experienced some of its most exciting days in connection with baseball: The 1909 Ijamsville Juniors were undefeated; the 1911 team gained the county championship; and in 1921, Ijamsville, though the smallest team in the Frederick County League, placed third.

Ijamsville also won pennants in the Maryland State League in 1939, 1942, 1949 and on into the '50s—1954, 1955, 1957 and 1958—plus the Shaughnessy playoff title in 1948, 1950, 1954, 1955 and 1958.

"Baseball was a big thing," says Sally Thomas, who lived on the Plummer Ijams' farm, part of the Paradise tract, in Ijamsville. "A lot of communities had a team. This baseball team was famous," she continues, "and almost like a farm team for the Orioles. There was a ball diamond called Moxley Field in town. Some of the Orioles would

The train station, early in the twentieth century. *Courtesy of the Historical Society of Frederick County.*

come and scout here with my Uncle Reg and Charlie Moylan. At an earlier time, my Aunt Fern did the bookkeeping for the 1911 winning ball club."

Mrs. Thomas points out that at one time quarrying and the railroad were very important to the community. It could hardly have been a quiet place, with rock powder blasts to loosen slate and the frequent passing of freight trains. According to retired postmaster Nelson "Bing" Myers, a lot of trains still pass through, twelve or fifteen a day, hauling coal from the west.

In 1821 the village was in fact named Ijam's Mill, when Plummer Ijams Jr., son of the area's first settler, granted right-of-way through his land to the B&O. But in June 1832, when the first post office opened, the town became Ijamsville, with Plummer Ijams the appointed postmaster.

Mr. Myers, one of Ijamsville's last postmasters, recalls that forty years ago, there were 390 rural boxes. "There are over 1,000 now," he says, "and several big businesses are within the rural route boundaries."

Ijamsville residents today receive their mail through Monrovia, with no address change.

Mr. Myers comments that the place is changing. Several developments have sprung up, and several more are planned. Already there is impact. "Traffic is terrible," he remarks. "I can sit on my porch on a Sunday evening and count six or seven cars a minute going by. Between five and eight in the morning, it's bumper-to-bumper traffic. People are driving to Washington or meeting carpools."

Traces of past activities of other kinds remain. At one railroad crossing (at Mussetter Road) are seen the shell of an old general store and the ruins of a long-abandoned gristmill. Near the other railroad crossing, at Ijamsville Road, is a pit now filled with water, where the desirable blue-green and purple phyllite slate was quarried until 1870. Many of the miners came from Wales, and on Saturday night, they and the local farmers would gather at the village stores. Frequently, the town constable had to be fetched to settle altercations.

Mr. Myers remembers when shale was quarried right behind the village, up until 1937. And he recalls the filling in of the other slate quarry a dozen or so years ago. "It was filled in with tires," he relates, "and covered over. There must be a million tires back there! Gabriel's restaurant, which was the hospital, is on one hill, the village is on the other, and the slate quarry was right in between.

"Conrad Hargett's house, completely covered with slate, is still here, but it's been remodeled, and now it's covered with aluminum siding," observes Mr. Myers.

In 1932, the 1877 schoolhouse was closed and, in 1936, purchased by the Methodist Episcopal Church next door. Its roof is made of original slate, as is the church's, on the south side.

In bygone times, English influence was evident in the town's architecture and manner; the King of England originally granted tracts of land in the area to a number of families, including the Ijams. That influence continued well into the present century. Mrs. Thomas says, "The village was more like an English village. In the '40s, Victorian houses were occupied mostly by widow ladies who had wonderful gardens. They would have tea parties, and the ladies invited would stroll through the garden, getting clippings to take home." Those present would reciprocate with teas of their own, and "specimens" would be gathered and replanted all over the town.

A roof of Ijamsville slate can be seen on the town's former schoolhouse, owned by the nearby church. *Photo by Ray S. Price.*

While that charm and gentility are part of a picture not likely to be seen again, the Ijamsville community is being enhanced by a new spirit of growth and energy—perhaps a not unwelcome change from its industries of the past.

—June 1990

Planes and Trains: How Mount Airy Made the Grade

"We get a lot of fresh air—and plenty of snow," says former Mount Airy postmaster Travis Norwood. Parr's Ridge at Mount Airy has the highest elevation between the seashore and the mountains in Maryland; at 825 feet, it is the "airiest" spot between Baltimore and Catoctin Mountain. Legend says that the town received its name on a cold and windy day when an Irish brakeman on the B&O Railroad made the comment, "The weather here is rather airish."

"Situated on the crest of Parr's Ridge, Mount Airy may be compared to ancient Rome, the city of seven hills," reads the little town's centennial book (1894–1994) with pride. The railroad was an important part of life in Mount Airy, circa 1900. "The residential sections of Mount Airy spread over several hills which completely surround the business and shopping district." Mount Airy is an attractive place, with an all-American appeal. The community's homes remind the former postmaster "of some of the houses in the south, in Charleston and Savannah," says Norwood. "Some there are bigger, of course!" he quickly adds.

This easternmost municipality is different from Frederick County's other eleven self-governing towns in that it is divided by a county line. Margaret (Routzahn) Miller now resides on the Braddock Heights ridge but has deep roots in her hometown of Mount Airy. She speaks of the two-county system: "I lived on South Main Street. I was in Carroll County, and the houses across the street were in Frederick County." Because of annexations in recent years, the fast-growing population is now about equally distributed between these counties.

Mount Airy is one of only two Frederick municipalities issuing its own building permits. Facilities are often shared by the two counties. When ground was broken for the new Mount Airy library and senior center at Parr's Ridge in 1991, three Frederick County commissioners were in attendance; they related that their county's contribution to the $2.6 million project was $200,000.

The last class to graduate from high school in Mount Airy was in 1967. Since then, students attend either South Carroll or Linganore (Frederick County) High School. But a regional school is a possibility for the future; the municipality's growth may warrant a new educational facility of its own.

When Lewis Dixon was mayor (1972–1986), an idea emerged to create a new county, called Linganore, from the bisected town. Parts of Frederick, Carroll, Montgomery and Howard Counties would have been included. Delegate Julien Delphey recalls introducing into the General Assembly in the 1970s a resolution to study this proposal. It went nowhere, no doubt in part because Mount Airy's town council members were unanimously against such a plan. The junction of the four counties is found in a pretty site not far from Mount Airy. A yellowed newspaper clipping from early in this century tells of the annual Mount Airy Farmers' Picnic held at Wildwood Park, "attended by thousands and is quite a mecca for politicians. The late Governor Warfield accepted his nomination for the Maryland governorship in this picturesque grove."

Oscar Baker, who grew up on a farm outside Mount Airy, knows the area well. "In 1946, I gave my wife a diamond in that park," he says. A few years ago, Mayor Gerald Johnson asked Baker to oversee a committee that worked with the town planner to look into possible locations for senior housing. The old parkland was selected, and it seems that Baker and his wife have come full circle, as they now comfortably reside in one of those units.

It was "the railroad that opened up Mount Airy," says Margaret Miller. In 1831, the B&O Railroad came to Ridgeville, and until 1839, horses moved the locomotives and cars up inclined steps, or planes, because of the steep grade. A community bearing the name Plane No. 4 is still on the map a few miles west of the municipality. In 1839, when a spur line came through what is now Mount Airy, the grade lessened by eighty or one hundred feet. Henry Bussard, the settlement's first resident, sold land for the railroad right-of-way, and he became the first station agent. Herman Beck, local historian of both town and railroad, has spoken of the 2,758-foot tunnel running under the planes. Completed in 1902, it was the longest railroad tunnel between Harpers Ferry, West Virginia, and Baltimore. Many of the construction crew were Irish or Black, and when the work was in progress in Ridgeville, two hundred or three hundred workers moved to the area. Mrs. Miller remembers that the trains made quite a comeback during World War II. But they stopped running in 1950.

Oscar Baker refers to a combination of railroad and small town atmosphere in Mount Airy. He describes what drew people, mostly farmers, from miles around to the place when he was growing up: "If anyone ordered machinery, it would come in by train. The first fire engine came on freight cars." A couple Sears and Roebuck houses, too, were

This devastating 1903 fire, followed by major fires in 1914 and 1925, led to the formation of the Mount Airy Volunteer Fire Department in 1926. *Courtesy of the Historical Society of Mount Airy, Maryland.*

delivered by rail. He tells of Saturday night band concerts but relays that the biggest enticement to be in Mount Airy on Saturday night was the drawing in front of what was then the Potomac Edison office. "Drawings brought droves of folks into town," says Baker. "During the week, if you bought things like produce at the stores, or furniture, you'd get a ticket that said ten percent or as much as fifty percent on it, if you bought a lot. If your name was drawn Saturday night, you'd get that percentage of the money. You had to be present to win. That's the reason there was such a big crowd in town."

The community has sprung back from three devastating conflagrations that swept the business district in 1903, 1914 and 1925 (when the June 4 temperature hit 103 degrees). Firefighting equipment in those years had to be hauled in from Frederick by train. Since the formation of Mount Airy Volunteer Fire Department in 1926, containment of blazes has been possible.

—June 1998, the year of
Frederick County's 250th anniversary celebration

"Dunkers" and "Dogtowns" Define Johnsville

It is not known how Johnsville got its name, but it has been implied that it was because so many of the inhabitants were named John; for example—John Kitterman, John Diggs, John Williams, John Chalmers, and later John Willits, John Knizer, John Myer, John Harmon, John Garber, John Merz, John Roberts, and John Wolfe." In 1976, Marie Burns, Ellen Wyatt and Sundra Funkhouser compiled a small book containing such nuggets of information about this Frederick County community located five miles from Union Bridge.

"As early as 1732," they found, "the land in this western wilderness was offered by the owner to encourage settlers. Any person having a family could settle on 200 acres without paying rent for three years, and any single person, male or female, between the ages of 15 and 30, could settle on 100 acres on the same terms."

To the original purchasers, the British Crown issued title to the land, under patents. It was English-speaking settlers who obtained the larger tracts of land and farmed them, using slaves. A well-known slave plantation near Johnsville was Warfield's Delight, the property of S.D. Warfield.

On the main route from Baltimore to the West, the settlement was at one time a comfortable stopover place for travelers. Many businesses, serving visitors and townsfolk alike, then flourished.

"The three toll gates which blocked the road from Johnsville to Frederick disappeared when the State put a hard-surfaced road through.

It used to be three cents for a horse and ten cents for a buggy. Broad tread tires went free but narrow tread wagons cost their owners eight cents," informs the little volume about the village.

Also of economic importance to the Johnsville area were its copper deposits. Opening before 1760 and in intermittent operation under different owners until 1918, the Liberty Mine shut down in 1918. According to a 1946 publication of the Department of Geology, Mines and Water Resources, State of Maryland, concentrates during the last years of activity are said to have averaged 24 percent copper and 1.3 cents silver, while the ore in 1907 reportedly averaged 2.16 percent copper, 4.7 ounces silver and $1.80 gold. "It has been said that some of the copper from this mine was used on the dome of the Capitol in Washington, D.C.," mentions the Johnsville book.

Among the sturdy pioneers in Johnsville District was the Iler family. Scharf's *History of Western Maryland* tells us that "the Ilers were noted for their numbers and fine physical development. Peter Iler, who died in 1872, aged seventy years, left nine sons and twelve girls, all strong and hearty men and women. Of these sons not one weighed less than one hundred and eighty pounds. Mr. Iler never had a physician in his house for any of his twenty-one children."

The religious denomination called Dunkers—German Baptists—was well represented in the area. The 1886 Frederick County directory describes them as "noted for their thrift, honesty, and good citizenship generally."

A section of a few houses on Maryland Route 75 at the edge of town is sometimes referred to as "Dogtown." "I don't know how it got that name," remarks Barbara Norris, now principal of Carroll Manor Elementary School, who was born in that little place with such a colorful designation. "I lived on a farm right below the hill there." She reminisced a moment about once being on a sleigh going through the main street of town. "You couldn't do that today," she says.

Among the community events that bring people out from miles around to socialize are the old-fashioned spring and fall dinners at the parish hall of the Johnsville United Methodist Church on Maryland Route 75. While a drive to the town is a pleasant experience anytime, enjoying the church dinner fellowship—the public is welcome—can afford a visitor a less superficial look at Johnsville, and one might soon find agreement with Ms. Norris as she says, "When I go through this little town, I have lots of warm memories."

—*June 1992*

Libertytown Wasn't Always Free

From general stores to privies and copper mines to disaster memorials, this village in eastern Frederick County is full of unique surprises. Its history also offers an interesting bit of irony—Libertytown and its district was once the largest slaveholding area in the county.

The town wasn't always known by its current name. The first survey in 1739 referred to the tract of six hundred acres, owned and laid out by John Young, as "Duke's Woods." The fledgling community attracted so many immigrants from England and Wales that people called the district "Little Britain."

Libertytown acquired its present name in 1782, but it isn't clear how. One story suggests Richard Coale, John Young's heir, inspired the name when he urged people to build in a place where they could "enjoy liberty." Other folks believe the hamlet gained its name in honor of the Sons of Liberty, a group of patriots in the colonies who organized on the eve of the American Revolution to oppose the British Stamp Act.

Travelers between Frederick and Baltimore found Libertytown a convenient place to rest during their journeys. It soon became a regular stop for stagecoaches and mail riders as well. Farmers driving their livestock and poultry to market along the town's dirt road, which followed an old Indian trail, would bed their animals down for the night in holding pens while they stayed at one of the area's taverns or inns. Wagonmasters parked their vehicles in the courtyards of the public houses.

John Wagner's tavern was the first in town. Ownership passed through a number of hands during the years. James Roberts, the son of a slave owned by the Coale family, lived in the old tavern into the 1920s.

"Libertytown was a very thriving town in its earliest years," notes retired schoolteacher and lifelong resident Ada Beall Poole. She can recall many businesses and professions from the town's past. One was Simpson's, a general store in existence at the intersection of Routes 26 and 75 since 1904. But Mrs. Poole says she patronized another store, owned by Milton Carter, located at the other end of town where she lived. She remembers picking out candy there, adding, "We'd get a couple of pieces of candy for a penny."

Perhaps due to the influence of Welsh immigrants, copper mining provided another important industry in the Liberty District. The most prominent operations included Liberty Copper Mine, New London Mine and the Dolly Hide Mine. Water seepage and other problems often hampered work, causing high production costs. The cost was warranted during the Civil War and again during the First World War when those conflicts drove up the price of the metal. But after World War I no further attempts were made to reactivate production.

The Tin Shop is just one of the many businesses from Libertytown's thriving past that has long since disappeared. *Courtesy of the Carl Brown Collection, FCPL.*

The hustle and bustle of the town's earlier years began to decline. Many of the old homes became victims of neglect; others, such as some of the log homes, hid beneath a remodeled facade. Mrs. Poole's property is perhaps unique because most of its original outbuildings have been retained. Entered from the kitchen door are the slave kitchen and smokehouse. Beyond stand a corncrib, chicken house and stable.

But the old outhouse has attracted special attention, since it is one of the few still in excellent condition that can be found in the area. (Mrs. Poole stresses that it is no longer in use.) Architecture students from the University of Maryland arrived on a field trip one day to study the tiny structure.

Another unique feature still visible to visitors is the memorial to the victims of the *Titanic* disaster, located in the cemetery of St. Peter's Catholic Church. This is supposed to be the first such remembrance of that tragic 1912 sinking erected anywhere. St. Peter's congregation itself dates back to 1821. Six years later, the Methodists constructed the Libertytown United Methodist Church on what had been the town's marketplace. Blacks attended the John Wesley Chapel of the Methodist Episcopal Church, which was in use from 1885 until 1970.

Libertytown turned down the opportunity to have the railroad come through town. Some residents, including Liberty High School principal Wallace R. Beall (Mrs. Poole's father), felt that moment marked the end of the town's growth. The rail line traveled through Woodsboro and Walkersville, about six miles away. "Both of those places have outstripped Libertytown," observes Mrs. Poole. But perhaps that quirk of fate spared this little hamlet on Route 26 the loss of its special character and charm.

—July 1993

New Market Is Known for Old Things

A longitudinal town, about six hundred feet wide and but half a mile long when first laid out, New Market was not always the antiques center we know today. Stores, undertaking establishments, blacksmith and wheelwright shops and many taverns and hotels once occupied the buildings that visitors now enter in search of treasures from the past.

Mrs. Alverta Falconer, ninety years old and a resident of Frederick, carries one of the oldest family names associated with the pretty village. Arriving from England in the 1700s, Falconers were cabinetmakers, house builders and undertakers. "In those days, people called them undertakers," says Mrs. Falconer. "Grandpa made all the baby caskets. They bought all the adult caskets. In the winter they made shutters, too. The boys helped their daddy [her husband], but didn't want to carry it on." There are no Falconers left in New Market now, but the many houses they built—some west of town and others in Mount Airy—remain standing.

During the sale at the closing of their undertaking business, New Market mayor Frank Shaw bought a number of items, including the surplus caskets. He put them into a storage area adjacent to his store, and his youngsters and other children in the neighborhood often played among them. One day, however, some customers wandered into that side room. An older lady happened to expose the viewing portion of one of the boxes. Shaw tells how "the lady passed right out. One of the kids had gotten into that coffin, and when she opened the panel, he was lying right there! I sold all the coffins after that."

Peace and Plenty, Help, Darby's Delight, Good Meadows, Hickory Plains and Hall's Choice are only a few of the colorful survey names for parcels and tracts of old estates in the New Market district. They belonged at one time to the estate of Mrs. Cordelia H. Downey, part of a family that acquired a great deal of land—some of which had been Downey-owned since the days of Lord Baltimore's first grant—by purchase and inheritance. The family of Dr. Hopkins owned much of the land close by.

People affectionately referred to the village as "Dr. Downey's Town" after Dr. Jesse W. Downey, for the land was included in what was known as New Market Plains when William Downey originally settled there in 1814. The district boasted the largest population of that period, and it was a slave-holding territory of considerable size as well.

Even before Nicholas Hall laid out the town in 1793, Samuel Plummer had built the first house in the area; it was known as "Plummer's part of New Market Plains," but it was George Smith who put up the first house, used as a tavern, in town after New Marker's final planning.

When Main Street became a section of the National Pike, travelers and herdsmen would pause for refreshment or overnight there, while journeying between Frederick and Baltimore. According to the *Frederick Post* of December 31, 1975, "Many of the town's existing antique shops and private dwellings date to the period between 1810 and 1830, when they served as hostels and taverns. The period's Federal architectural style still dominates the streetscape of New Market, but a progression through the Greek Revival and Victorian styles is also obvious…Only eight or ten of the original buildings in New Market have been razed since their construction."

Longtime resident Paul Zimmerman remembers that five houses of worship were once part of the community. Three remain—Grace Episcopal, New Market United Methodist and Simpson Methodist Churches.

Folger McKenzie, the Bentztown bard, wrote in his column in the *Sun* (Baltimore) September 24, 1941, of old New Market institutions long gone, such as the blacksmith shop, the band and the baseball team. He also told of the stopover places so important to travelers: "None of the old taverns that once formed so picturesque a phase of the life of old

The Utz hotel, predecessor of New Market's landmark Mealey's Inn, had no front porch. *Private collection.*

New Market now exist, but Mealey's Hotel on Main Street in the center of town is a relic of stagecoach days and is a landmark of the place. It was once one of the old taverns, and opposite it were two others, while two more flourished farther west along the road."

"My husband said there was either mud on New Market streets or deep dust, all summer," Mrs. Falconer recalls. "The porches would be full of dust. There were stepping stones—flagstones—across the street. The state laid blacktop quite early." Here she pauses and says she has an anecdote about that. A certain wealthy man nearby "liked the ladies. He would spend the weekend with different ones at Mealey's Hotel." Because of the poor condition of the street, he saw to it that just that portion adjacent to the hotel received several truckloads of blacktop. "It was a big wide spot right in from of the hotel," she says. "People believed he was instrumental in pushing the state to blacktop the whole street."

The *1886 General Directory of Frederick County* described New Market succinctly: "Blessed with pure water, good hygiene, pure air and good

Isaac Russell, wheelwright, was New Market's first mayor, 1878–1880. *Private collection.*

crops, it is a pleasant place to live." On the National Register of Historic Places, this former haven for travelers has become a most agreeable attraction for present-day tourists as well.

—May 1991

Bartonsville Has "All the Magic!"

While rapid growth and development are becoming a way of life in the southern end of Frederick County, a drive down Bartonsville Road just three miles southeast of Frederick leads to a still-small and friendly community. A few modest residences front the road, the oldest of which may conceal original log cabin construction beneath the modern siding and shingles. Both former schoolhouses—one for black youngsters, the other for white—remain in use as homes, and Bartonsville's two churches continue an old tradition of providing a spiritual focus for the tiny village's handful of residents.

Greensberry Barton probably would feel right at home—and even recognize a few names—if he could visit his namesake community today. It was just prior to the Civil War when the former slave bought a piece of land here from a Mr. Miller and built his home on it. As the first permanent resident of this part of the New Market District, Barton was no doubt pleased to have the new village carry his name.

Another early settler and ex-slave was William Orange Brooks, who came to Bartonsville after the War Between the States. His grandson, Charles Brooks, still calls this place home.

Cato Adams, also a freed slave, played an important role in the hamlet's history. His name appears on the August 24, 1878 deed for land on which a "building for worship" was to be constructed. According to Nina Honemond Clarke's *History of the Nineteenth Century Black Churches in Maryland and Washington, D.C.*, "The church was dedicated October 12, 1879. It has undergone many changes, both physical and spiritual… Even the name has been changed. First it was known as Jackson Chapel, then Jackson Methodist Episcopal Church, and now Jackson United Methodist Church."

A rift occurred in the congregation, although the exact cause has been forgotten. "Something or other happened, and we split," explains longtime resident Alice Hill, referring to the incident that took place before she was born. Another house of worship, St. James A.M.E. Church, was founded a few years later. It celebrated its centennial in 1983. The church continues to serve the community's religious needs and remains about the only prominent landmark in the town.

Other institutions that were part of Bartonsville's more lively past have disappeared. Once relatively self-sufficient, with a general store, a grocery, a gas station and even a dance hall, those who now live here must head toward Frederick for shopping and entertainment.

For decades, the name Hamilton and the word "store" were practically synonymous for Bartonsville and adjacent Pearl residents. Frederick diarist Jacob Engelbrecht noted in his entry for November 3, 1870 that "we made sauerkraut today from 29 heads of cabbage (small ones), and 23 we got from the son of Mr. John Hamilton in Bartonsville at 4 cents a head, and 6 I bought at market afterwards."

Later, Minnie J. Hamilton was the proprietor of a general store at nearby Pearl, according to the 1885 city and county directory.

Hill recalls that the Pearl Bargain House closed in the early 1940s because of anticipated roadwork, and Hamilton then opened a market in Frederick, but the route of the new Jug Bridge approach road was changed.

Eikers, Guariglias and Mealeys all owned small grocery stores in the village.

Harry Main made history in 1934 when he opened here the first full-service filling station outside of Frederick. Gasoline sold for twenty-nine cents a gallon. He continued in business for forty years.

Early in Bartonsville's history a fraternal order known as the Working Man's Society formed to provide assistance with burials. Eventually, this organization became the Galilean Fishermen. They built the dance hall, now fallen down, at the intersection of Bartonsville and Tobery roads, which also served as their meeting place. Weekly dances drew residents from all over Frederick County. John Ross's Nighthawks and the Iantha Orchestra, two popular bands, always attracted large crowds. On Labor Day 1930, Lester Bowie Sr., Bemon Hill (Alice Hill's husband) and John Tyler staged the county's first midnight dance in that hall. It became a successful tradition. Funds from the late-night dances provided a clay tennis court for the community.

Music played an important part in the community. The Bartonsville Cornet Band carried the name throughout the county and now around the world, thanks to a musician with local roots. A 1915 photograph of the band appears on the cover of trumpeter Lester Bowie Jr.'s 1983 ECM recording "All The Magic!" Bowie, a founding member of the Art Ensemble of Chicago and leader of such groups as Brass Fantasy, has three uncles in that historic picture. His father, Lester Bowie Sr., joined the cornet band as a boy. Lester's father, now retired from a long career as

Legacies live on: the 1915 Bartonsville Cornet Band appears on the cover of a record album by jazz trumpeter Lester Bowie Jr., who has three uncles in the photo. *Courtesy of Belva King.*

a music teacher, and his aunt, Edna Bowie Dykes, also a retired educator, still reside in Bartonsville, as do musician siblings Joe, a trombonist with his band Defunkt, and Byron, a saxophonist and arranger. The brothers and their father live in a contemporary family dwelling on the site of the old log family home where so much talent was nourished.

—*October 1993*

West

The Pop Shop of Feagaville

Country music plays from a local station on the general store's small radio, appropriate background for friendly exchange between proprietor James Feaga and folks who stop by. The ding and jingle of the opening door punctuate their arrival in a place that time has overlooked, and one almost expects to see rosy-cheeked farm youngsters grouped outside for recess in the schoolyard just up the road. But the Feagaville school closed in 1940, and the construction workers who drive up in their tool-laden pickup trucks for noon-time sandwiches and soda jolt away the nostalgia.

"This pretty, neat and thrifty town is situated on the Frederick and Jefferson Pike, about three miles west of the city of Frederick, in the county of the same name." An apt description, it actually appears in a book about local people published before the turn of the century.

It can probably be claimed that Feagaville is the most frequently mispronounced place name in the county. Derived from a descendant of Johann Phillip Fiege, a Hessian soldier, the name underwent a spelling change with a long-ago error in a legal document, while pronunciation remained essentially the same: "Figgy" is pretty close.

Thinking that the locale looked a lot like Germany, early landseekers decided to stay. Although generally thought that Cullers were first to settle here—and the name remains prominent to this day—the town became Feagaville, not Red Spring or Cullerville, with the coming of the post office in 1885. Charles Edward Feaga, only son of a miller who operated the old Frederick Mills and termed the town's "most active and aggressive inhabitant," was foremost in persuading the government, with a widely circulated petition, of the need for that federal service, and Feaga himself was declared postmaster.

While the post office is long gone, the business begun also in 1885 by farmer turned merchant Feaga is not only still thriving, but the Pop Shop is also the center of this tiny community of two streets. Run by the founder's grandson, James H. Feaga, it has outlasted by nearly fifty years the only competition it ever had. "Yes, Arthur Culler opened a store in the '30s in the red brick house up on the corner," recalls Mr. Feaga. "He gave us a fit for a while. Culler finally sold the property, and the new owner called my dad to see if he wanted to buy it. He did."

The Ballenger Community Hall, at one time an adequate two-room school for area children, is also a gathering place for grange meetings, suppers and receptions.

To Diana Droneburg Fox-Holter, whose parents owned Feagaville's well-known Fruit Factory featuring local produce, "It's all changed now.

Heart of the community—Feagaville's centenarian Pop Shop. *Photo by Ray S. Price.*

It used to be a close-knit community. Feaga's and the farmers are all the same. Cullers are holding on to their land. And some of the people on Feagaville Lane have been there forever—but a lot of people have passed away or moved away."

Third-generation James Feaga says, too, "It's all changed so much. I used to know everybody who lived here. There isn't any of the old ones left anymore." Remarking on how many strangers he sees, Feaga comments, "The discount sodas, the discount chips and the gasoline bring people from all around. I sell two truckloads of gas in a week; a lot of contractors buy their fuel here."

Portrait photographs of three generations of Feagas hang in the store. Missing is a comparable likeness of Jimmy Feaga, of whom his dad says, "He just hated to have his picture made." It was not destined that Jimmy should take over the business, as he passed away suddenly and unexpectedly May 30, 1989, at the age of forty, to the shock of the entire community. One feels, however, that Mr. Feaga's younger helper, Adam, of whom the elderly gentleman speaks warmly and highly, may be just the person to keep the Pop Shop bustling in the future. Turning seventy-three this month and reflecting on his own mortality, he speaks of his request that the store be open the day after he is buried. "I serve a lot of people around here, and I don't want to lose the regular customers."

The reasons Dianna's parents moved to Feagaville are still valid for families seeking to locate anew: the quiet and the nice people. Maybe the clock can't be turned back to the Friday and Saturday nights of yesteryear when the farmers would come by Feaga's store to get groceries, sip a soda and chat. But life still tends to move at a slower pace in this unincorporated town of some one hundred souls—and a lot of folks would like to keep it that way.

—March 1990

Horsey Whiskey: The Pride of Burkittsville

A little horse paperweight recently showed up at a sale. Carl Brown, a local history buff employed in C. Burr Artz Library's Maryland Room, picked up the handsome object and turned it over. "I saw the name Outerbridge Horsey Distillery on the bottom," he says, "and didn't think anyone there would know anything about it." Prepared to bid fifty dollars for the piece, he was astonished when it went for several hundred dollars.

Mr. Horsey's distillery, founded in 1850, produced whiskey that enjoyed a national reputation. Made from pure South Mountain water, it traveled thousands of miles from Burkittsville to acquire that fame. Scharf's *History of Western Maryland* (originally published in 1882) relates that the largest whiskey orders

> *come from New York, Boston, Chicago, Cincinnati, and the State of California. Nothing, it is said, gives such flavor and tone to whisky as age, aided by a sea voyage. Once made it is placed in the bonded warehouse, remaining in an even temperature, for months, often years, after which it is shipped to the seaboard, and thence around Cape Horn to the Pacific coast, where it remains for a year or two, after which it is brought back, rich in all the qualities that epicures require.*

Baltimore was the place of reentry.

Sam Crone, Burkittsville retiree and manager of the village's community center, tells that "the distillery burned during the Civil War. Confederate and Union troops came through. The Confederates got whiskey, got drunk and burned it down—all the buildings. It was rebuilt."

Another time, a daring robbery of a considerable quantity of the distillery's famous product implicated two prominent Frederick citizens.

The great financial success of Mr. Horsey's business prompted Mr. Ahalt to convert his nearby mill, originally erected as a gristmill, into a distillery, which was also successful.

Prohibition became the law in 1920, and the government came to close Mr. Horsey down. A guard, a man not known for moderation where hard spirits were concerned, according to Mr. Crone, "was posted to keep people from getting at the whiskey before it could be disposed of the next day. The fellow drank all he could. Townspeople sent Dr. Yurdy [one of two local physicians] there with horse and buggy to get some of the whiskey out before the Feds destroyed it. [The unsteady guard] made out that he didn't recognize him, and he shot and killed Dr. Yurdy. The townspeople didn't get any whiskey. The Feds came back and they poured it all out."

On Maryland Route 17, as one heads toward Brunswick, the name Horsey remains prominent on the landscape: "Ole Horsey Distillery Farm" proclaims the sign in front of the property where stands the large original Horsey home. It is no longer owned by the distillery family.

Mr. Crone, formerly a school bus driver, mentions that the old Horsey school for "colored" children was also nearby. He recalls, "The school was getting pretty bad [run-down], and then desegregation came," and the youngsters moved to the Burkittsville school. Horsey School, converted into a private residence, still occupies a knoll by the highway. Built in 1914, Burkittsville School closed in the spring of 1968, when consolidation occurred. A year later, Sam Crone served on the Ruritan committee that purchased the still sturdy structure, which has been adaptively reused. Community functions take place there, and garment manufacturer Deva rents the entire basement. The Jefferson school was sold to a developer in the '69 sale; it was torn down.

Main Street, Burkittsville, is an example of successful historic preservation. *Photo by Ray S. Price.*

Upon entering Burkittsville, one notices a sign informing that the town was established in 1812. Originally called Harley's Post Office, it was later renamed for Henry Burkitt, a prominent landowner, whose grave is tucked away there in a small, private cemetery. Burkitt's imposing home, built in 1807, can be seen on Main Street. It remains one of the recommended sights on the walking tour outlined by the Burkittsville District Heritage Society.

In 1975, the entire community was put on the National Register of Historic Places. Change occurs almost imperceptibly in Burkittsville.

Mr. Harley operated the first store in town. Several other general stores have come and gone. Nowadays people shop at area supermarkets.

Burkittsville witnessed the Civil War Battle of Crampton's Gap on September 13 and 14, 1862. Mrs. Josephine Harley found herself busy baking during that time: twenty-one loaves of bread and eighteen pies from her kitchen were eaten by Confederates. Wiener's tannery had to give up forty-five new saddles to the troops.

Grapes cultivated on land where part of the fighting took place go to Montgomery County. It seems in keeping with the village's reputation for famous beverages that this present-day product travels some miles to become part of Catoctin Vineyard's selection of award-winning wines.

Wear walking shoes, bring a camera or sketchpad and plan to explore this nineteenth-century townscape. It's a picturesque and charming portrait of America's past.

—*April 1991*

Jefferson: A Rowdy Stringtown No More

New Town, Trap, Traptown, Newtown Trap—all these names and more were, in the early 1800s, applied to the place Frederick Countians have long known as Jefferson. The third platted town in the county, it came into being on November 15, 1774, when a deed transferred ninety-eight acres of land—"Lowland" tract—to Mrs. Eleanore Madley, who had the town formally laid out.

The village's unsavory reputation gave rise to such terms as Trap and Newtown Trap. According to Scharf's *History of Western Maryland*, journeying through this "rough and dangerous settlement" was a risky business. Waylaying and robbing of a traveler there was a common occurrence, and taverns and gambling also relieved those passing through of their money. While many of the townsfolk wanted to call the fledgling community Catoctin, after the Indians that once lived in the fertile valley, it was the respected elder citizen Dr. Charles MacGill who gave "Trap" a more dignified designation. Because he admired Thomas Jefferson, the doctor chose to name the village after the country's third president.

Thanks to the efforts of Representative Thomas Cost Johnson, the 1831–32 legislature incorporated the town and made the name official. A descendant of Maryland's first governor, he is buried in Jefferson's Lutheran cemetery.

During the eighteenth and nineteenth centuries, it was common practice in Western Maryland to "string out" a town on both sides of a road. In 1775, Elias De Lashmutt founded a twenty-lot community called New Freedom opposite New Town, thereby forming a "stringtown" with his property, plus that of Mrs. Madley's.

Jefferson's Main Street (Maryland Route 180) was formerly a busy, bustling turnpike—Jefferson Pike. Bentztown bard Folger McKinsey, in a column fifty years ago, described it as the "through road between the North and South, and coaches and teams and horsemen and foot travelers were constantly on the move here from one direction or another."

A hundred years ago, Jefferson boasted three stores and five churches. St. Paul's Lutheran Church earlier this year celebrated 150 years of continuous ministry at the same location.

Mrs. Gertiline Nichols, eighty-seven years old, remembers another church in Jefferson: "I went to grade school in the church. Mr. McKinney was the teacher. I started there when I was eight and went there for three years. Then it was closed, but the building was still used as the colored church." She adds, "It was near the beginning of the town as you came from Middletown." When it was closed and torn down, her family attended Sunnyside Church.

Williams's *History of Frederick County, Maryland* includes a passage, quoted in the Ruritan's bicentennial book, *Jefferson 1774–1974*, about this church, built there before the Civil War for slaves' use. "A writer complained in January 1854 in a letter to the Frederick Examiner of the Negro church in Jefferson. In essence [the writer] complained…services were held nightly until very late hours…felt the young Negro fellows congregate there to arrange plans for mischief and rascality…and [this, the writer claimed] had a demoralizing effect on the young Negroes." The book goes on to say that "the editor of the Examiner agreed with the writer and further pointed out that the 'Act of Assembly of 1831 made it unlawful for Negroes to attend religious services unless conducted by an ordained minister or authorized by a white person.'"

Jefferson's lack of compliance with terms of incorporation resulted in its being "untowned" by legislative act. Henry Culler served as the first mayor. Folger McKinsey noted that the woman's club had a big role in raising funds for public improvements, such as paving and lights.

Between 1907 and 1943, the Hagerstown and Frederick (H&F) Railway went to Jefferson, but the planned link between that line and the B&O steam system in Brunswick never materialized.

The Hagerstown and Frederick Railway enters Jefferson from the east in this early twentieth-century view. *Courtesy of the Historical Society of Frederick County.*

Hemp's Meats, opened in 1848 by Abraham Hemp, has remained in the hands of the same family and has thrived and grown. Hemp's no doubt witnessed the century-ago turkey drives through town—and perhaps added the bird to its meat display. Starting at daybreak from Knoxville, turkey drivers would herd flocks of gobblers by the hundreds through Jefferson, en route to markets in Frederick and even Baltimore and Washington.

Another business opened its doors in 1848—the Etchison Funeral Home; it moved to Frederick in 1922. "Julia Etchison Hana's father had the funeral home," recalls eighty-five-year-old Frederick resident Arnold Delauter. "If somebody died in Pleasant View, Mr. Etchison would come and embalm right in the house and put the body into the coffin. The family would sit up all night until the funeral. Mr. Etchison would take the body to church and to the Point of Rocks cemetery." Mr. Delauter adds, "It would take all day to have a funeral." Fixed in his memory is the sight of Mr. Etchison, dressed all in black, sitting up high in the roofless driver's seat of the carriage, with the horses moving at a dignified pace.

Lewis Mill, the community's oldest structure, still stands and is now the home of Catoctin Pottery, serving as a wonderful example of adaptive reuse of a truly historic building. According to *Jefferson 1774–1974*:

the waters of the Catoctin Creek operated many water-powered mills throughout the area. These mill sites were generally the meeting places for neighboring farmers and their friends. The millers were thought to be wealthy, and many loaned money to farmers. As an old German farmer would say, "the millers' hogs were always the fattest." On many occasions crimes ranging from thievery to murder were committed at these mills.

But few places could be safer than present-day Jefferson. Not only is this "stringtown" a nice place to visit, people will tell you it's a nice place to live.

—*August 1991*

Living in Harmony

For Clarence Ford, now seventy-nine years old, the dream of most schoolchildren came true one morning in 1921: the schoolhouse in his small town of Harmony burned to the ground.

"I remember seeing a big cloud of smoke," says Ford, who attended the rebuilt Harmony school through the seventh grade. In the 1930s, Harmony school ceased to exist entirely when the schools in the area were consolidated into one in Middletown. Ford recalls many a cold ride to school from his home in Harmony by horse and buggy with his cousin Maynard.

Harmony is nine miles west of Frederick, about one-quarter of a mile north of U.S. Route 40 near Myersville. The village is nestled in a pretty valley on Little Catoctin Creek. Originally called Beallsville, the community was established in the early nineteenth century around one of the area's first mills. Confused with another "Beallsville" in the state, the name was changed to Harmony.

Harmony was at one time virtually self-sufficient. The center of activity would have been at the intersection of Brethren Church, Harmony and Hollow Roads. Ford's home was at the northwest corner of this crossroads. A 2.5-story stone and brick building, it dates to 1840 when it was established as a gristmill.

The Ford home was first converted from a gristmill to a woolen factory that produced coverlets now highly prized by collectors. Clarence's father,

Charlie, converted the first floor of the mill into a general store and the second floor into their home in 1924. Clarence Ford took over operation of the store after World War II and immediately purchased the area's first television set. "When I got out of the Navy, I went to the American Television Laboratory and learned 'TV.' I bought the parts and assembled one, hung it up on a shelf in the store, and people would sit there and watch it."

Harmony is famous for its music traditions. The Harmony Cornet Band has been in existence for seventy-eight years, and nearly every resident in the area has been involved in the band in some way. The community hall—where the band's weekly rehearsals take place—is the circa 1906 former Reformed Church building. Neighbors in nearby Fisher's Hollow were also musical and made music together, such as Clarence Ford on guitar and Phil Fisher on the fiddle. The duo performed together in the 1940s at the dance hall on Gas House Pike.

Other amusements in Harmony included festivals, picnics and church socials. Baseball used to be a big deal in Harmony too. A team from Harmony participated in the Frederick County League for many years.

Old-time Harmony residents still speak of a local character called "Buffalo Bill"—Robert Ridgely. The schoolteacher and preacher had

The Cornet Band has been at the center of the community since its organization in 1916. *Courtesy of the Harmony Cornet Band.*

long flowing hair, a full mustache and a flowing beard. He made it his mission to take to the hills on his horse searching for whiskey stills. Ridgely reported them to the authorities. Despite his unpopular pastime, Ridgely survived into retirement in Myersville.

Harmony's latest local legend is ninety-year-old "Aunt Mary" Leatherman who made local headlines last summer celebrating her birthday with a long-dreamed of helicopter ride, declaring the experience "wonderful."

—*October 1995*

Duking It Out in Battletown

On August 23, 1833, Jacob Englebrecht made the following entry in his diary:

> *Having curiosity to ascertain the number of houses in Frederick I took the trouble to count them…I found the town to contain 867 houses fronting on streets including stables at public houses and that the northern part of town up from Patrick St. is 470 alone. The addition to town commonly called Battle Town containing 18 houses is not in the above enumeration but properly should be as by an act of the last legislature it is embraced in the corporation.*

Colonel Stephen Steiner, who designed and built the Trinity Chapel steeple on West Church Street, and Stephen Ramsburg laid out this community at the west end of downtown Frederick's Patrick Street; its earliest resident was a Stephen Klein. People first called the section Stephensville, but it was not long before the place earned the title "Ratsville," presumably because of a large rodent population. A dispute involving Colonel Steiner and Mr. Klein gave rise to the neighborhood's third name—Battletown.

Around the turn of the century, Dr. Charles Hoffman wrote that "the addition, being outside of the corporate limits of Frederick town, became the frequent resort of parties who wished to have a fight without interruption by the authorities," a fact that doubtless reinforced the combative title.

The former residence of Colonel Steiner still stands on the summit of what used to be called "Bentztown Hill." At present, the Frederick Woman's Civic Club owns this handsome 1807 brick structure, located at 368 West Patrick Street. In the early part of this century, the building functioned as a beer saloon.

Another popular establishment shared the hill with Steiner's house. According to *Frederick: A Pictorial History*, "the old stone tavern in 'Battletown,' at the corner of Patrick Street and Telegraph (now Jefferson) Street was built around 1800, prior to the opening of the National Road. Builder and owner was a Mr. Bowers. The tavern was a haven for Henry Clay, Andrew Jackson, and Daniel Webster when they traveled on the National Road."

Frederick resident Margaret Kent, eighty-six, recalls that her great-grandfather, Dr. Josiah Kline, a Rocky Ridge veterinarian who cared for

The tavern at the corner of Patrick and Telegraph (now Jefferson) Streets attracted visitors like Henry Clay, Andrew Jackson and Daniel Webster. It was razed in the 1920s. *Courtesy of the Historical Society of Frederick County.*

Union officers' horses, moved his family to the old stone structure when her grandmother was just six years old.

Unfortunately, the landmark no longer exists. Referring to the sale of the historic building to the Gulf Oil Company in the 1920s, Miss Kent describes the subsequent demolition as a "great tragedy," happening before people realized what was going on. Today, Ken's Automotive Transmission Specialties is located where the Gulf filling station once stood.

While many of the neighborhood's earliest inhabitants were of German background, a number of black families also joined the community. Fredericktonian Gladys Brown Lee believes her great-grandmother, Caroline Nelson Tyson, was the first person of color who owned property in Battletown, "where Fredericktown Bank is now."

A quarry owned by Bernie Winkle, sometimes called "the tire man," stretched all the way from Telegraph (Jefferson) Street down to Carroll Creek. He later filled the hole with Model T Fords from his junkyard, and the city used it as a landfill, according to eighty-year-old Lord Nickens, whose family moved to the corner of South and Telegraph Streets in 1919. Houses were built over the site.

Nickens remembers, "Mr. Bowie had a miniature golf course in his yard—for blacks." It opened in the 1930s at 452 West Patrick Street. Later, the A&P bought Mr. Bowie's land and built a store; Frederick Cablevision now occupies the property.

Carl Brown tells of Bernie Winkle's various enterprises in Battletown, including a used car lot and the arena where fights—cockfights, too—were held.

But the most popular place of all was Mr. Winkle's club—Hollywood Gardens—for black entertainment. Among the big names who performed there were Cab Calloway, Lionel Hampton and Ella Fitzgerald.

—*March 1993*

Myersville Is Perfect in Every Way

"Few towns can offer more inducements as a place of residence… healthfulness, a beautiful town and a still more beautiful country surrounding it, a pleasant climate, economy in living…schools, churches in abundance, a sociable, cultivated and hospitable people, always ready to welcome strangers, accessibility and proximity to the national capital and other large cities." While these lines so complimentary to the village came from Ira C. Moser's 1905 *History of Myersville*, they ring no less true today. Published by the *Myersville Monitor*, Moser's writing, in quaintly phrased English, extolled the community's good health: "The high situation of Myersville, its distance from water and the pure mountain air of the valley combine to make the town remarkably healthy. Not one death is known that resulted from contagious diseases directly from the climate."

Regarded at one time as a popular summer resort boasting a comfortable hotel—the Shank House—Myersville no doubt appealed to vacationers both because of its renowned pure air and water and its outstanding location near Catoctin Creek, thirteen miles from Frederick and thirteen miles from Hagerstown.

Scharf's *History of Western Maryland* describes the village as "filled with enterprising mechanics, and it is the chief seat of trade for a populous country for miles around."

Mr. Moser's account of the goings-on at the grog shop in the stable of George Toms and John Young, however, indicates that things were not always quiet in Myersville: "This place was the scene of most disgraceful conduct, brawls, etc., every night, especially on Saturday nights. This continued for years, and [it] was named the 'old lick.'" Other such establishments followed, and gambling was rampant. One enterprising proprietor also happened to be town magistrate; he sold the liquor one day and fined his drunken customers on the next! Some prominent citizens introduced reforms, and when Upton Buhrman gained a seat in the Maryland legislature in 1864, he was successful in getting a local option law passed "prohibiting the sale of intoxicating liquors within three miles of the churches of Myersville."

The little community, incorporated in 1904, also earned the reputation of being an unsavory place when elections were held. Early in the twentieth century, a thief made off with the ballot box. Sheriff Otho Gaver caught the culprit in Frederick and marched him back to the scene of the crime, box in hand, with the officer of the law close behind on horseback, urging the fellow along. According to the town's updated [to 1971] history, "at election time it's been said that Myersville got as rough as Kentucky, and that during elections a bushel basket of revolvers was ready in Buhrman's store."

Main Street runs the length of the village, and a number of older structures fronting the thoroughfare have survived. Upon this road operated the trolleys of the Hagerstown and Frederick Railway. In 1898, the newly built street car system connected with Frederick and, in 1904, with Hagerstown. For decades an important means of transportation, by 1945 it was no longer needed; the tracks came up, and blacktop was laid down. Gil Stroup, who has served as mayor here, recalls riding the trolley daily for four years while he attended Middletown High School. A favorite Sunday excursion for families was a trolley trip to Braddock Heights, eight miles away, for a picnic and recreation.

Another Myersville resident sometimes arrived at school in a more unusual way. "I lived on a farm outside of town," says Margaret Dutrow, a retired schoolteacher. "I didn't ride the horse to school every day," she explains, "but only when the weather was bad. My uncle took me [on the horse]. I was a little girl, in the first grade."

Most of the settlement's early arrivals were German immigrants. Myers is an old name in the area, and the community became known as Myersville, although the family was not the first to move into the peaceful

A postcard view of Main Street shows three transportation options: trolley, road or sidewalk. *Courtesy of the Historical Society of Frederick County.*

wilderness of Middletown Valley. Gradually, the German language and culture disappeared. In remembrance of this heritage, St. John's Lutheran Church, on Church Hill Road at Myersville, celebrated its 200th anniversary in May 1990 with one worship service conducted partly in German. Parishioners were invited to attend this special gathering dressed as people might have been two centuries earlier.

The charm of Myersville endures. One resident went so far as to state: "Myersville doesn't need improvement; it's perfect in every way."

—*March 1992*

Beware the Snallygaster's Lair in Middletown

The Snallygaster first put in his appearance flying over South Mountain from Middletown and was first seen by Charles F. Main and Ed McLighter in the vicinity of Braddock Heights. He was of portentous size and shape and emitted the most bloodcurdling noises. His creator told me that after having him dangle before the imaginations of readers of the Register *for some time, he finally buried him in a liquor vat at Mount Briar, Washington County, for this was in the days when moonshining had become a major industry.*

Thus reminisced Folger McKinsey, the Bentztown bard, in his *Baltimore Sun* column of December 12, 1938, about Middletown's most famous inhabitant and said furthermore that he bowed "in especial respect to the world-famed Snallygaster, who put in his appearance over the town in 1932 and created a much-more-than-nine-days' wonder. He was apparently the twin brother of the famous Vovolapus, created I believe, in the fertile imagination of the late 'Dick' Hamilton, of Hagerstown. I met and shook hands while here with the creator of the Snallygaster. He is Ralph S. Wolfe Sr., news editor of the *Valley Register*."

Liquor vat notwithstanding, occasional sightings, particularly by partygoers, of a bizarre flying creature are still reported from this part of Frederick County, sixty years after the Snallygaster's initial viewing.

Middletown, in the heart of the picturesque Middletown Valley, is literally a place in the middle, located near Middle Creek, equally distant from the Catoctin and Blue Ridge Mountains. It is also eight miles away from both Frederick City and Boonsboro, in Washington County.

Frederick Stemple and Jacob Lorentz are said to be Middletown's first settlers. In 1834, the community became incorporated; Jacob Hoffman took office as first burgess. Present burgess Louise Snodgrass is the first woman to be elected head of the town's government.

While Scharf's *History of Western Maryland* tells that the settlement "was laid out just after the close of the Revolution by Margaret Crone, who owned the land on which the town now stands," an article in the *Frederick Post* of November 7, 1972, took issue with this claim, repeated as well in Williams's *History of Frederick County*. Millard Milburn Rice describes the statement that "Middletown was laid out on a tract of land called Smithfield, which derived its name from a gunsmith shop built on it in 1730 by one Frederick Lauber" as not true, according to Frederick County court, land and will records. That account shows that platting was done nine years before the Declaration of Independence. Margaret Crone would have been a small child or not yet born at that time, as she lived to at least the year 1839.

George Rhoderick included in his book The Early History of Middletown, Maryland both versions of Middletown's origin but seemed partial to Rice's painstaking research, which apparently refuted the story about Margaret Crone.

While the lovely old Victorian homes that line Middletown's shaded Main Street are a major attraction, and many residents in the entire Washington area have pleasant memories of Main's Ice Cream, a walk up Jefferson Street will give the visitor a glimpse of a yet earlier time in the community's past. Former Middletown Valley Historical Society president George Brigham Jr. describes that section as one of the oldest parts of town, with the oldest being in the vicinity of the Gladhill Furniture Company building:

"That [Jefferson] was the street, the main drag, to Burkittsville. Route 17 wasn't there. At the farthest end of Jefferson Street was the colored community. It was of moderate size." According to Washington Conference records—a church body that existed from 1928 to 1954—the Asbury Methodist Episcopal Church on Jefferson Street was

The most dramatic difference a visitor to Middletown today would notice is the style of automobiles parked along the street. *Courtesy of the Historical Society of Frederick County.*

active from 1868 until the late '30s. President of the Frederick County Chapter of the NAACP, Lord Nickens, recalls that the small stone church was torn down. Its footings are still visible, and thanks to the ambitious Eagle Scout project of Middletown resident Bryan Hanes, the abandoned cemetery site, once a mass of tangled undergrowth is now just about cleared. "The [local] churches had been asking the scouts to clean it out," says Bryan. It took two days of work by thirty-five Boy Scouts. "And we aren't really finished yet. We're going to have the fire department burn out the rest of the brush, and then we'll reseed." George Brigham remarks, "The history there ought to be deeply researched."

One source mentions as well a black community called "Africa" west of Middletown. Also west of the town used to be Bowlus's mill and cotton factory, near what was referred to as "Spoolsville."

The historic home of Dr. Lamar, who tended to the medical needs of the townspeople early in this century, still stands at 200 West Main Street. The turn-of-the-century operating and recovery rooms and the doctor's books and records have survived; the property has in the past been open periodically for tours. It remains in private ownership.

Once boasting a movie theater, Middletown was easy to reach by trolley or automobile. The sport of horseracing was also at one time popular in Frederick County and enjoyed in Middletown as well. Scharf's history tells us that "on Sept. 20, 21, and 22, 1809, races were run at Middletown, with John Stottlemire and Jonathan Levy as managers; entrance, 'one shilling in the pound.'" Now, instead of a dirt track for horses, we find a paved one at the Middletown Raceway, for operating radio-controlled model race cars.

It was reported that during the fighting on South Mountain, a Civil War general climbed to the top of the steeple of Middletown's Lutheran church to observe the movements of the troops. The three-year-old Central Maryland Heritage League is trying to preserve this piece of history. It is steadily receiving $25 checks from individuals wishing to purchase one-square-foot parcels of land where twenty-five thousand Union and ten thousand Confederate troops fought the Battle of South Mountain September 14, 1862. The first purchaser was Representative Beverly Byron. The league has five years in which to pay off $325,000 the land trust used to buy twenty-two acres at the battle's site. Support is coming from such far-flung places as California, New York, Virginia, Puerto Rico, the Washington, D.C. area and Tokyo, according to George Brigham. Letters about relatives who took part in the battle accompany some of the donations. Local Civil War enthusiasts look forward to holding mountainside reenactments there.

—May 1992, the year that Middletown, founded in 1767, celebrated its 225th anniversary

Always on the Sunnyside

Conard Hawker emphasizes that the little community's name is actually Mountville, explaining, "It was the name of the post office…in the same building with the store. Sunnyside came in when they built the colored schoolhouse here. People called it Sunnyside because it was on the sunny side of the mountain."

Mr. Hawker, nearing eighty, grew up on Mountville Road. Several generations of Hawkers operated a grocery store there. He mentions, "There was a store in that location before the Civil War. Mrs. Hankey ran that store. It sold to Perry Waskey. His son Charles was postmaster and ran the store. RFD [Rural Free Delivery] came in around 1908 or 1910. When the Mountville post office closed, Charles took the job as postmaster at Lander."

According to the bicentennial book, *Jefferson: 1774–1974*, most of Mountville's homes "were built of logs hewed by hand. There were two grocery stores and a dry goods store. The school house was built in 1888. At the present time, it is used as the community hall." It still is. But the businesses operated by Charlotte Basford, Henry King and the Hawkers are gone.

The description continues: "The first people who settled in the community of Sunnyside were mostly slaves. They first held church services in private houses. In 1885 they built their first chapel. It was located on what is now Basford Road and Mountville Road, but at that time was known as Bridle Road."

Families pooled their resources to build the Sunnyside United Methodist Church. Gravestones here bear the names of some of those early benefactors. *Photo by Davis Hall.*

By the early 1900s, according to Mr. Hawker, Mountville had achieved a fifty-fifty racial balance between black and white residents. "The church started in 1899," he says, referring to the Sunnyside United Methodist Church. Those who purchased the land for a place of worship included Jacob and Ellen McKinney, George and Ellen Jones, John and Ellen Weedon, George and Caroline Nickolas and Joseph Shorter. They donated an acre to the community for a school building and a cemetery as well.

Weedons have made up a large part of the population in the vicinity. John Thomas Weedon, formerly a slave in Licksville, was the first of that family to settle as a free man in what was called Mountville. During the Civil War, it was not uncommon for runaway slaves to seek refuge at Union army camps. Such was the case with Weedon, who escaped his slaveholder and worked as a mule driver for Union troops. A 1979 Frederick *News-Post* article quoted grandson Oscar Weedon: "When the fighting was through, John returned to Licksville and got his wife and child. With the money he had saved, John took his family to Sunnyside and bought a piece of land, which made him the first Weedon in the community."

Mr. Hawker tells of a tiny black settlement once nestled on the other side of Mountville. People called it Halltown, for Nathan Hall, who, with his wife, Sally, had fled from slavery. Other families there were the (Henry) Thomases, Prices, Whitens, Herberts and (Dan) Halls. Folks would walk or ride in wagons from Halltown to Sunnyside or Jefferson to obtain the few goods and services they could not themselves provide, such as blacksmithing.

Mrs. Ardella Young, almost ninety-two, was born and raised in Halltown. She remembers that while there was always plenty to eat, people in the village did not have a lot of worldly possessions. She says, "All of us girls would wear the same dress to school on Monday, and when Friday came we would take the dress off. On Saturday we would wash our dresses and hang them up to dry. Then Sunday morning we would put that same dress on to go to Sunday school and church. And we'd wear that same dress to school on Monday."

Generations of Frederick County schoolchildren, participating in the outdoor school program, share Mrs. Young's memories of a prominent rocky feature on the mountain: A stay at Mar-Lu Ridge camp, off Mountville Road, always included a visit to Buzzard Rock, with its thirty-foot dropoff on one side and a small cave beneath. Mrs. Young recalls that climbing there as a child was "like going up stairs," and she terms this amusement "our Sunday evening pleasure," remembering how the Halltown youngsters took delight in looking around from that elevation.

One need not take a long hike to find an interesting view. The casual weekend explorer of Frederick County's byways can pause for a bit of "Sunday pleasure" in gazing from Mountville toward Adamstown, even from the church and community center grounds and reflect on this area's rich history.

—February 1992

Rosemont Stands Up for Itself

Mention Rosemont, and you're likely to hear, "Where's that?" North of Brunswick, this village in the county's southwestern section earned a spot on the map as a municipality almost forty years ago, thanks to folks who wanted to preserve the community's quality of life.

In the winter of 1953, Emory Frye, president of the Bank of Brunswick and a Rosemont resident, learned from a Southern States board member of a threat to the tranquility of the little place: The Brunswick Cooperative Association had made plans to build a new feed and grain mill on the hamlet's southern edge. Since no local or county zoning regulations existed to protect the settlement, civic-minded residents met to determine how best to approach the problem of possible commercial development. Following trips by citizens bearing a petition signed by dozens of property owners to Annapolis and Frederick for the purpose of discussing a plan of action with elected officials, attorney James McSherry outlined the procedure for what the citizen group needed to do—incorporate.

"I'll never forget that," says Mrs. Elizabeth Frye of their efforts. The first meeting took place in her living room. "Those five men came in here when the plans to become a municipality were discussed."

The *Frederick Post* of April 21, 1972, reported in an article about Rosemont's history that "a motion was presented [to the Maryland Legislature] by Charles Gross that legislation be introduced at once incorporating the village of Rosemont in order that a zoning and planning commission might be established to effect the orderly development of the village. That was seconded by Dr. J.G.F. Smith and passed by unanimous vote."

Charles Gross, Ralph Stauffer and B. Harwood Watson paid the county farm agent's office the required fifteen-dollar fee to prepare a map of Rosemont.

The governor delayed in signing the bill. The co-op continued to press for the site selected. But incorporation at last took effect. The new mill came up in Brunswick. "There were no hard feelings" about the change in location, according to Mrs. Frye.

Voters in the first election after incorporation, held May 2,1953, chose John T. Graham as burgess. John Votipka currently holds that office. Thus Rosemont became the smallest municipality in Frederick County; it is next door to the second-largest, Brunswick.

A couple businesses operate out of houses and do not intrude on the area's pleasant residential character. Twenty years ago, the Christian and Missionary Alliance Church came into the village. The community continues to consist of individually built houses and attractive yards, on lots that were once part of several farms until the early 1900s.

Rosemont resident Ada Bartlett stands in the road in front of her home, a pleasantly quiet spot in 1949. *Courtesy of Vicki Torbert.*

"There are very few [people] left from fifty years ago," remarks Mrs. Frye. She points across the street to where Dr. Smith, who practiced medicine in Brunswick, lived, and she reveals that his home was a frame, top-of-the-line Sears house. "He came here in 1915...built the Sears house in the '20s. It's been bricked and a side porch added." The residence has had two new owners since Dr. Smith died. Mrs. Frye adds that there were many Sears houses in Brunswick; the railroad brought them in.

Village treasurer Mary Ann Mauzy gives the current population of Rosemont as 256, with the number of houses approximately one hundred. The Brunswick water system serves some residents, while the rest are on wells. Mail comes via Knoxville. The ten cents on every one hundred dollars of assessed property has remained constant, and revenue takes care of streetlights and contributions to the Brunswick Senior Citizens Center, as well as fire and rescue services from that neighboring town.

Calling Rosemont "a neat community" besides being quiet, Mrs. Frye concludes by saying, "Well, I tell you—I can sit on that back porch and look across the countryside, and as yet it's still country. There have been a number of people who would like to develop that land out there, but I can still sit and enjoy the view that I have."

—September 1992

Lock 29 Lands You in Lander

When I was a kid, we used to fish in the canal," says Louise Horman. "There was enough water then for fishing, but later it went dry." For many years, her grandparents lived in the lockhouse at Lander, by Chesapeake and Ohio (C&O) Canal lift lock no. 29—Catoctin Lock. Mrs. Horman's grandfather, Lewis Henry "Bugs" Cross, came into the world on the canal boat owned by his father, and her mother was born in Two Lacks Lockhouse, west of Harper's Ferry.

Until flooding in 1924 caused considerable damage to the C&O Canal, Cross captained a boat hauling coal from Cumberland to Washington, D.C. As that era of transportation came to an end, many families whose lives were an intimate part of this waterway had to seek other ways of earning a living. "When the canal closed," tells Mrs. Horman, "my grandfather stayed right at the river and began his business of renting and caring for boats."

Between lock no. 29 and the river stands a thick growth of trees. A hike or drive of several hundred yards down a rutted and often puddle-filled road leads to the edge of the Potomac River. Earlier in this century, no trees blocked the view from canal or railroad to river. Some folks recall that Jim Pearl farmed those bottomlands—and the community's baseball diamond was a prominent feature on that landscape. Along the Potomac stood cabins, but after being swept away in a flood, they were never replaced.

This Historic American Buildings Survey photo shows the Lander lock number 29, now part of the Chesapeake and Ohio National Historical Park. *Courtesy of the Library of Congress.*

"Those floods were something," remarks Mrs. Horman, who witnessed as a child the biggest one on record, in 1936, when water lapped at the lockhouse's second story. "I can remember going up and down the railroad tracks in a boat. We all had to take those typhoid shots. They were the worst shots I ever had."

The settlement always has been small, with farming the main occupation, and dwellings situated mostly along Lander Road. Its railroad station was called Catoctin. Located sixteen miles from Frederick, near Jefferson, this tiny Baltimore and Ohio (B&O) office received at one time four mails a day. Waskey's store, founded in 1912 and in operation until 1966, and the post office, closed in 1958, shared the same little building; a partition separated them. Mrs. Horman's aunts ran them both for many years. "I used to help my aunts pack those mail sacks," she recalls and describes how "they were hung on the mailcatcher, which was reached by ascending a short iron ladder. As the train thundered by, an iron arm extended out and picked the sack from the catcher. In exchange, another sack filled with mail for our community would be tossed out along the track in front of the post office."

The father of former Frederick County commissioner Charles Smith was born in Lander and farmed nearby. "My dad used to take milk to the railroad siding with a horse and wagon," says Smith, a Jefferson resident. He speaks fondly of the old general store, with its big potbellied stove—a place to gather and chat.

Memories of Lander go back to early childhood for Frederick resident Arnold Delauter, eighty-six, who took the train from Doubs to visit his grandmother, Annie Delauter. He also had an aunt and uncle who worked in Lander for twenty years on the Fawley farm.

In the early days, Lander area children attended Union School, built in 1824. According to the *Frederick County Directory of 1886*, "Some 40 or 50 years ago the school was one of the finest in the county." Latin and Greek were part of the curriculum.

Effie Hind Roderuck, now one hundred years old and residing at Homewood, was the last of fourteen children of a C&O canal boatman and a schoolteacher. While her siblings received their education at Union School, she tells of entering the new school at Lander, which had one room for seven grades. This building still stands, remodeled as a residence.

A favorite Lander reminiscence for Mrs. Horman is the annual "excursion." She recalls: "We'd get about sixteen kids—cousins would come over from Frederick—and we'd walk on the towpath to Brunswick. We'd take along hot dogs and build a fire along the way and roast them. Then we'd catch what we called 'the little Tonnerville' back to Lander. That was our summer pleasure. It wasn't costly. We enjoyed simple pleasures."

—*November 1992*

From Berlin to Brunswick, a Railroad Town Finds Its Name

It is one of the most unusual towns in the State…built upon terraced slopes, and its background is a green ridge of mountain peak, along the very top of which, almost, sites have been chosen for building. Even the High School is located way up there against the skyline, and there are whole streets of attractive cottages, where occupants are able to look westward toward the Virginias and down upon the broad waters of the Potomac." So wrote Bentztown bard Folger McKinsey about Brunswick in 1938. The town had appeared that way, however, for less than fifty years, situated until 1890 on a spread of land between the foothills and the Potomac River.

A canal town since the arrival of the Chesapeake and Ohio (C&O) Company in 1834, served also since that year by the Baltimore and Ohio (B&O) Railroad, Berlin (as people called the village from 1787) attracted the attention of B&O officials. Ideal topography as well as a location convenient to the junctions of Harpers Ferry, Point of Rocks and Weverton made Berlin a suitable site for a new freight classification and storage yard of considerable size. B&O representatives, seeking to acquire land necessary for such an undertaking at the most reasonable cost, came to the village disguised as farmers. Feigning interest in the fertile floodplain, they were able to purchase all the land needed, and the company thus shifted its freight yard from Martinsburg, West Virginia, to this new area twenty-five miles away.

C&O Canal lock house 30 in Brunswick is marooned by the 1924 flood. *Courtesy of the Brunswick Railroad Museum.*

Because another Maryland town also bore the name Berlin (many settlers had come from Berlin, Germany), and since a railroad official requested a "fancy" name for this important place, Brunswick became the chosen appellation, no doubt influenced by the many townspeople from Brunswick, Germany. On April 8, 1890, the Maryland legislature passed an enabling act to incorporate the settlement and change its name.

Brunswick came last in a whole string of names for the village, some both descriptive and colorful, among them Eel Town, Buffalo Wallow, German Crossing and Hawkins' Merry Peep O'Day.

The new designation obviously pleased the local people, for the first child born in Brunswick, on May 11, 1890, was named Martha Brunswick Sigafoose (Van Osdale), and the parents of the first twins, born April 24, 1891, called the pair Lula Brunswick and Luther Brunswick Darr.

The following decade witnessed much expansion and tremendous growth in population. And the impressive freight yard, over 7 miles long and boasting 130 miles of track, was touted as the largest in America owned by a single company.

John Hawkins began to operate a ferry there. Later, a covered bridge carried travelers from Brunswick to Loudoun County.

Folger McKinsey described the place in its "Berlin" period as "one of the liveliest canal communities between Georgetown and Cumberland."

The village was not entirely German in character, for many Irish migrated there to work and live while building the canal. With many black families, too, railroading became a tradition. Retired railroader—and member of the Brunswick History Commission—George Hardy recalls that he drove a school bus before getting a job with the railroad in the early 1930s. "I was the first black disposition clerk, siding clerk and demurrage (car record) clerk," he says.

According to Mary Margrabe, another member of the Brunswick History Commission, the town went on record in 1956 as the first in Frederick County to desegregate its schools. Board of Education employee Teresa Harris remembers how an unexpected act of nature launched the integration process, when "an electrical storm started a fire in the old Brunswick [colored] school." Harris's mother recounts that parents didn't want the damaged schoolhouse on J Street, already run-down before the fire, to be repaired. So Teresa's sister, then nearly six years old, was among the first children to enter an integrated classroom.

Throughout the Civil War, both canal and railroad made the village a focus of military activity, and troops of both sides crossed the river there.

During World War II, Brunswick again became a potential target, with a record 101,000 cars per month passing through the rail yard. The government stationed anti-aircraft watchers on the hills to scan the skies for possible German aircraft.

"Singing auctioneer" Anne-Lynn Gross speaks of her hometown: "The railroad's the biggest thing in Brunswick. I grew up practically on top of the tracks. My father's store was right next to the tracks. People would get off the train and do their shopping."

The town now owns the renovated one-hundred-year-old train station, designed by architect E. Francis Baldwin, as well as the only roundhouse in the state. Adding to Brunswick's uniqueness is the national park within its boundaries, between the C&O canal and the river—and the National Park Service plans to restore a one-mile stretch there of the historic water transportation system.

Is the railroad history enough to keep tourists coming to Brunswick? "The old flavor of Brunswick still exists," says Gross. "I'd love to see

Working on the railroad about 1906. *Courtesy of the Brunswick Railroad Museum.*

the return of mom-and-pop businesses that would be an attraction to tourists—where you'd get personalized treatment. Some of the new businesses have that basic philosophy, but restoring it fully would take a while."

—November 1991

Selected Bibliography

Brugger, Robert J. *Maryland, A Middle Temperament: 1634–1980*. Baltimore, MD: JHU Press, 1996.

Clarke, Nina Honemond. *History of the Nineteenth Century Black Churches in Maryland and Washington, D.C.* New York: Vantage Press, 1983.

Engelbrecht, Jacob. *The Diary of Jacob Englebrecht, Historical Society of Frederick County, Inc*. Frederick, MD: Historical Society of Frederick County, 1976.

Gordon, Paul and Rita. *A Textbook History of Frederick County, Board of Education of Frederick County, MD*. Frederick, MD: Board of Education of Frederick County, 1975.

Lake, D.J. *Atlas of Frederick County, Maryland*. Philadelphia, PA: C.O. Titus and Co., 1873.

Miller, Chas. W. (compiled by). *General Directory of Frederick City, Frederick, MD*. Frederick, MD: W.T. Delaplaine, 1886.

Scharf, J. Thomas. *History of Western Maryland, Being a History of Frederick, Montgomery, Carroll, Washington, Allegany, and Garrett Counties from the Earliest*

Period to the Present Day; Including Biographical Sketches of Their Representative Men, 2 Volumes. Philadelphia, PA: L.H. Everts, 1882.

Schildknecht, Calvin. E. *Monocacy and Catoctin*, Volume I. Shippensburg, PA: Beidel Printing House, 1985.

Whitmore, Nancy F., and Timothy L. Cannon. *Frederick, A Pictorial History*. Norfolk, VA: Donning Co., 1981.

Williams, T.J.C. *History of Frederick County Maryland*. Frederick, MD: L.R. Titsworth and Co., 1910.

Newspaper references include the *Washington Post*, *Baltimore News*, *Frederick News-Post*, *Myersville Monitor*, *Valley Register* (Middletown), and the *Blade-Times* (Brunswick).

Often quoted is Folger McKinsey, the Bentztown Bard, who wrote a column for the *Baltimore Sun* newspaper five days a week from 1906 until illness incapacitated him in 1948.

Other valuable resources include booklets published by churches, civic organizations and historical societies, including: Walkersville, Maryland: The Tale of Two Villages (1977); History and Legends of Urbana District (1976); Memories of Kemptown (1989); Tracey and Dern's Pioneers of Old Monocacy (1987); Reverend A.L. Oerter's History of Graceham; and Rhoderick's The Early History of Middletown, Maryland (1989).

Work by local historians includes Carl Brown's *Harmony Grove Recollections* (1990); Burns, Wyatt and Funhouser's *Johnsville: An Historic Review* (1976); Charles Moylan's *Ijamsville: The Story of a Country Village* (reprinted from the *Frederick News* in 1951); William J. Grove's *History of Carrollton Manor* (1922); Nancy Bodmer's *Buckey's Town: A Village Remembered* (1984); Martin and Rose's *The History of Wolfsville and the Catoctin District* (1972); Jay N. Ballentine Jr.'s *Jefferson 1774–1974* (1974); Millard Millburn Rice's *New Facts and Old Families* (1976); Nakhleh's *Emmitsburg: History and Society* (1976); *The History of Myersville* by Ira C. Moser (1905); and

Francis Smith's *Woodsboro Remembers: The History of Woodsboro from Its Beginning to 1976* (1976).

Readers inspired to research Frederick County history further will find all the publications listed here and more in the Maryland Room in the C. Burr Artz Library or at the Historical Society of Frederick County. Both outstanding archives are located in historic downtown Frederick.

About the Author

Author Marie Anne Erickson. *Photo courtesy of the* Frederick News-Post.

Born September 5, 1932, in Aurora, Illinois, Marie Anne Erickson was an only child of Swedish immigrants. She earned a bachelor's degree from the University of Nebraska, where she continued with graduate studies in zoology and foreign languages. After moving to the Frederick area in 1967, her interest in local history, the performing arts and everyone she met led to a long and prolific career as a writer. Her articles appeared in *Frederick Magazine* (formerly *Diversions*), the *Frederick News-Post*, the *Saxophone Journal*, *Bluegrass Unlimited*, the *Gazette* and other publications. She wrote the text for the original edition of the African American Heritage Sites tour brochure for the Tourism Council of Frederick County and is one of the historians interviewed in the documentary film *Up From the Meadows*, which chronicles the African American journey in Maryland. She served for many years as a judge for the Harry L. Decker Historical Essay Contest, which encourages fourth-graders to explore their local heritage. In 2007, the Tourism Council honored her as that year's Ambassador of Frederick.

Her trademark beret and tote bag full of notebooks, articles and photos, as well as her astonishing memory, are familiar to many Frederick residents. She remembered the name, face and story of each and every person she met.

As she neared her seventy-ninth birthday, Erickson was busy planning her next article. She died of complications from a stroke on September 3, 2011.

About the Editor

Although Ingrid Price has called New York City home for over thirty years, she thinks of Frederick as her hometown. The older daughter of Marie Anne Erickson and Ray S. Price, Ingrid wanted to become an anthropologist but accidentally earned a degree in theater from Florida State University instead. She is now a costume designer for film and television and recently produced a short film with husband Davis Hall. Assembling *Frederick County Chronicles: The Crossroads of Maryland* as a tribute to her late mother provided the unexpected joy of rediscovering the place where she grew up.